LOVE THAT LEVITATES

FINDING LOVE IN A LONELY GENERATION

DEANNA BLOCK

WestBow
PRESS®
A DIVISION OF THOMAS NELSON
& ZONDERVAN

WestBow Press books may be ordered through booksellers or by contacting:

WestBow Press
A Division of Thomas Nelson & Zondervan
1663 Liberty Drive
Bloomington, IN 47403
www.westbowpress.com
844-714-3454

ISBN: 978-1-6642-4753-6 (sc)
ISBN: 978-1-6642-4754-3 (hc)
ISBN: 978-1-6642-4752-9 (e)

Library of Congress Control Number: 2021921237

Print information available on the last page.

WestBow Press rev. date: 11/10/2021

CONTENTS

Introduction...vii

Chapter 1	Defining Love	1
Chapter 2	FOMO Fo-Sho..	7
Chapter 3	I Mean I'm Kind...	16
Chapter 4	My Heart Bleeds Red, But My Eyes See Green	24
Chapter 5	Help! I've Fallen And I Can't Get Up..........	29
Chapter 6	Feeling Bloated? It's Your Salty Self.............	36
Chapter 7	I Love You, But I Like Me More...................	43
Chapter 8	I Fight Like a Girl......................................	50
Chapter 9	Rude Attitude...	55
Chapter 10	The Devil Made Me Do It...........................	61
Chapter 11	I Win, You Lose..	66
Chapter 12	The Truth...	73
Chapter 13	The Whole Truth	81
Chapter 14	Nothing but the Truth................................	86
Chapter 15	So Help Me God	92
Chapter 16	Before, for Now, and Ever..........................	99

Notes 105

About the Author...109

INTRODUCTION

I never aspired to be a writer, and even though I am writing this with my book finished, I don't feel qualified to carry that title. I am just a girl with a lot of questions who enjoys the therapy of writing.

When I look back at 2020, my heart sinks. The election was a war that divided us, and coronavirus was the sickness that separated us. Families and friends battled on the field of opinion with no regard for the opposition.

We as a culture have put being right over being kind and loving. If someone isn't on our side, we dismiss him or her. If some people don't share our views, we berate them. We've stopped giving people the right to their opinions in conversation and instead treat discussions like verbal boxing matches. We've lost respect for one another.

I get it—I've been in discussions that make me irate. I've let my emotions steer the conversation when others' words felt like personal attacks. I have left a loving attitude behind and tried to justify my views. I didn't realize the importance of my attitude and tone while stating personal truths. I have often forgotten the gravity that my words and actions carry.

I wrote this book knowing that some readers won't share my views; I didn't write it to try to convince them. I wrote it to prompt discussion and give insight into thoughts others may have never pondered.

I hope as a nation we can find our way back to loving each other. Perhaps this book can enlighten and challenge you on the subject of love the way it has for me.

CHAPTER 1

DEFINING LOVE

What is love? Google dictionary says, "an intense feeling of deep affection," "a great interest and pleasure in something."[1] Haven't feelings led so many people astray though? They can be here one minute and gone the next. What happens when we don't feel deep affection or take an interest in something anymore? Was that love ever real?

One of Merriam-Webster's definitions of love seems to get off the surface describing "unselfish loyal and benevolent concern for the good of another."[2] It seems according to this definition that love is not only an action but also a reaction that stems from your character. *Benevolent* is a word that speaks positively and directly about the nature of a thing being good. As for being unselfish and loyal, it is rare to find a relationship defined by those attributes because loving like that requires hard, persistent work.

Society tells us to love ourselves first—that others can wait. Give loyalty only when it benefits us. What are the results of that attitude? Living lonely.

The *Washington Post* released an article in May 2018 titled, "Why Are Young Adults the Loneliest Generation in America?" In it, Rachel Simmons looked at a study released by a health company. The research showed that our nation's young adults, those between eighteen and twenty-two, were more isolated and disconnected than were our elderly. Looking into this article, I expected to see that screen time was the culprit, which the author later admitted didn't help. Instead, she suggested that the students she talked with weren't spending time alone. However, when they were around people, the connections stayed surface level.

She offered a list of what parents could do to help their college students.

1. Encourage them to take self-care seriously.
2. Remind them that everyone gets lonely sometimes.
3. Tell them that loneliness isn't their fault.[3]

I agree that it isn't always our fault when we feel lonely, but don't we play a part in it? Maybe we are a lonely generation because we allow ourselves to be lazy in relationships. The era we live in puts pressure on prestige. It is saturated with social media, making connection easier than ever, but it can't replace face-to-face communication. Deep down, we feel lonelier because we feel unknown.

Echosmith's song "Lonely Generation" states it like this.

> Here we are, left behind
> Looking through a screen makes you feel alright.
> Another day, another dime
> Looking in the wrong place for something right.
> We're a lonely generation
> A pixelated version of ourselves
> Empty conversations
> I've disconnected, now I'm by myself.[4]

Have you ever taken a break from social media? I have. I spent a lot more time working on building significant relationships. Hopefully, the lyrics "I've disconnected, now I'm by myself" are not true of us. Social media can give us a false sense of friendship. Friends who I thought would show up for me while I was on my social media break never even noticed I had left. We have empty conversations because there was never any real conversing.

As humans, we crave attention, affection, and admiration. These three needs can be seemingly met on social media. We know as women that sex sells, and you don't have to dig very deep to notice that when you flash a sexy selfie, it gets more attention than "real" posts. People like looking at the fantasy, and if you're honest, you'll admit that you like seeing yourself that way too. I don't think there is anything wrong with taking care of yourself; I'm a cosmetologist for goodness' sake! I want people to feel good about themselves and their images. But I also want people to know that they hold value internally. External beauty fades as we get older, but internal beauty has the potential to get better with time.

Our brains tell us that the more likes we have on social media, the more liked we are, but the truth is that the more likes we have, the more we've appealed to our audiences. Hey, good job advertising for you! The problem is that no matter how much we share in the caption, they don't truly know us, and that's why we still feel lonely. It's a pixelated version of ourselves, and it isn't enough. Likes may give us a mood boost, but how about that positive affirmation someone just DM'ed or dropped in the comments? Game changer. Conversation matters, and words have direct effect; even small gestures of communication can help give a relationship more depth.

On one of my Instagram with my high school girlfriends, I wrote the caption "So connected, I could be their Wi-Fi." There was a time when that was true about all of them. Honestly, looking at the post later, I realized it was not true for all of them now. I had not even talked meaningfully with one of the girls in years! Someone asked me one day what her career was, and I couldn't remember. I thought, *I don't have her on social media, so I don't know what's going on in her life.* It was aggravating how lazy I had become in a relationship that meant so much to me at one time. It dissolved because of my unwillingness to reach out just as much as hers.

Relationships are two-way streets. There are times when we try to reach out and restore a connection but the other person doesn't want to. Relationships take effort and time, but we aren't willing to invest that, so we hit the easy street of scroll city.

One time when I was being interviewed over the phone, the guy asked me what my Instagram name was. He looked me up, and as he was scrolling through my page, he said, "It looks like you have three kids. What are their ages?" It was a weird feeling to have him see who I and my family were before I'd ever met him. Forget about putting your best foot forward in a new relationship; you better have a good social media presence because that's where they have spent the last fifteen minutes getting to know you. We live in a virtual world. If we don't learn to disconnect from a filtered screen, how can we reconnect with reality? If love is what connects us in relationships, doesn't our definition of love matter the most?

In 1 John 4:8 (NIV), we read, "Whoever does not love does not know God, because God is love." Does love exist only if God exists? God's love for us is the central theme in the Bible, so how does it define love? I want to explore the biblical definition, and I ask you to contemplate whether this is truly the fullest definition, and if so, why.

> Love is patient, love is kind. It does not envy, it does not boast, it is not proud. It does not dishonor others, it is not self-seeking, it is not easily angered, it keeps not record of wrongs. Love does not delight in evil but rejoices with the truth. It always protects, it always trusts, always hopes, always perseveres. Love never fails. (1 Corinthians 13:4–8 NIV)

I began this personal journey when being questioned about my faith. I had never even thought to ask some of these questions. I grew up in a home that taught love existed because God existed. But what if God didn't exist? Science says that we need love to exist, but why's that? All things seem to serve a purpose, but what is a human's purpose? If this all happened by chance, why does it seem to have order and fit together so beautifully?

My mind spun for days during this time of searching. I did not let anyone into the struggle. I pushed people who loved me away because I didn't believe their love was genuine. I started forming opinions in my mind like, *They love me only if they can get what they want from me. If they really knew me, they wouldn't love me.* I bought the lie that I had to present myself as others wanted to see me for them to love me. I started seeking perfection, but the load was impossible to bear. I am a wild-child rebel, and coloring inside the lines is not my cup of tea. I'm creative, and I love adventure, so doing what I'm told for no apparent reason doesn't sit well with me. What if there were a reason to do the right thing though?

I am basing the foundation for this book on love because that is the place where I began to find the tangible truths that bonded my heart and mind. This is a part of my story and my journey, but it's also sprinkled with others' stories. I believe that even when our lives differ, we have some major commonalities and can learn from one another's experiences if we listen.

I believe you are beautiful and have a purpose, and I don't have to hear your story or see your face to know that. I'm here to try to prove to you that my statement is true. I don't want you to be alone. I want to stand by you and hold your hand in this journey of doubt and questioning. I hope this book helps you find answers to your questions. I hope that in the end, you will find the love and acceptance you've been made to crave.

CHAPTER 2

FOMO FO-SHO

(Love Is Patient)

I lack patience. In true millennial form, I want what I want and now. Waiting means I have no real control over the situation. We hustle our way through life checking off our goals and staring our achievements. Everyone is so busy, and we're not willing to make time to stop and smell the roses. We prioritize and quickly cut out simple interaction with others for productive days. I know that because I've lived that, and I can't say it works well. If my schedule is packed, I feel overwhelmed and too anxious to eat. If there's free time, I feel I'm not doing anything with my life.

The moments we spend with each other, even just in conversation, are meaningful. My kids do not need theme parks and expensive gifts as much as they need time with me. Uninterrupted togetherness chases the lonely away. It says that you are worth my time and attention and that you matter to me.

To be good friends with others and love well, we must practice patience with one another. Our behavior at a particular moment does not always speak directly to who we are but to how we are feeling. For example, if I am trying to accomplish a task and my three children ask me for something and I say, "Not right now," they persist, so I raise my voice and show my frustration. Would you say that I am an angry person? Maybe you would, or maybe you would look with understanding eyes and say that my kids met me at a time when I was already feeling overwhelmed and my response mirrored that. My kids were being impatient, and instead of showing them how to act, I reacted with the emotion I was telling them to suppress.

A better way to handle it would've been for me to explain to them how I was feeling and to ask them to join me in being patient. And as a parent, I have to have honest conversations with my kids and apologize for any of my harsh reactions. I acknowledge my faults and work on correcting them instead of excusing them so they don't become character traits.

Psalm 103:8 (NLT) says, "The Lord is merciful and compassionate, slow to get angry and filled with unfailing love." Jesus is the example I want to follow. He knows we are not perfect. He gently comes beside us willing to meet us right where we are. It takes patient love to see the best in others when they are acting their worst, but God asks us to have the same patience for others that He has for us. Patience is a response that speaks about our inner nature.

After high school, I left home and got a degree in cosmetology. Hair school was something else. Take high school, add adulting in four different age groups, and you have enough drama to make Hollywood salivate.

During the second month of school, an unfortunate rumor was spread about me. Much to my surprise, everyone believed it. I was very naïve back then. I thought that everyone would just naturally believe the best about me unless I gave them reason not to. Time taught me that some people would rather believe the worst instead of the best about others.

The rumor had pushed others away and sent me into isolation. I sat alone, I ate alone, I did life at school alone. During this time, I prayed for the Lord to defend me; I needed a friend, but it seemed that my words fell flat on heaven's doors. In the past, I had always had friends and loved ones supporting me, but they all felt so far away at that point.

One morning, I questioned why my character and beliefs were being attacked, and Matthew 5:44 (ESV) came to me: "Love your enemies and pray for those who persecute you." It was obvious to me what God wanted me to do, but I did not want to do it; I wanted to stand up for myself. I was hurt and angry. Thoughts of negating another's character to justify mine crossed my mind, but I saw how counterproductive that would be. If I wanted to be different, I would have to act in a way that represented that. I remember saying that I was sorry over and over as they walked away. Even though I didn't understand their anger, I wanted to, but they didn't want my apology.

After the discussion, I walked into the classroom to hear myself as the topic of conversation. I ran out of the class and climbed the stairs to an attic. As I sat in a corner, tears streamed down my face. This was the loneliest I had ever been. Hiding felt good for a while until I realized no one was coming to look for me. So I called home—a place I knew I was loved.

I told my mom that I wanted to quit school. I was done; this was too hard. She asked me why, and my mind was screaming, *Because I'm lonely!* but I told her, "Because I hate it." The truth sounded so weak and juvenile to me, so I lied. Just like God didn't give me the answer I wanted to hear, my mom didn't either. Looking back, I'm so glad she was the one to answer the phone that day.

My mom is my pusher, and my dad will usually let off if I blink my teary blue eyes in his direction. Those two were my perfect storm, and I needed both to mold and shape me. That moment though called for my mom. She told me, "You can do this, Deanna. Don't quit now. You have only ten months left. Just keep working hard and you'll be done before you know it."

Uhhh, ten months? I thought. *That's too long. I want to be done now!*

After we bantered back and forth a bit, she concluded, "Deanna, you're not quitting just because it's hard. You have an apartment with roommates who are counting on you to help with the rent. You've already spent everything you have to pay for this school, and you cannot get that back. You're going to finish what you started."

I was silent as anger began to rise up in me. My mom was supposed to be on my side. She had no idea what I was going through. After a few moments of silence, she said, "I better go. Hang in there. I love you."

I sat there for a while after mulling over what she had said and concluded that I didn't want to lose the money or disappoint my roommates. I cleaned myself up, snuck out the back door, and waited until my reentry wouldn't look suspicious. A few of the teachers asked me where I had gone, and I made up a lie about forgetting something at home.

After about four uncomfortable months, things started to change. I found comfort in the Lord as I read about how He conducted Himself while facing adversity. My anger started to subside, and I did not feel as alone. God did not send a friend to fight for me; He worked on my heart and character and told me to wait. While I waited, the Holy Spirit, the friend I had in me, got to work.

I started to examine the love of God and use it tangibly, and my classmates started seeing that perhaps what was presented to them about me was false. This is not even close to how my story usually goes; it was against my character to act that way. I want justice to be served in an instant until I'm the one on trial. Forgiveness started when I realized that I had been the offended and the offender. I am not better than anyone and have been the one to say horrible things about people out of anger or jealousy. I have been the one in need of grace and mercy.

Romans 12:17–18 (ESV) reads, "Repay no one evil for evil, but do what is honorable in the sight of all. If it is possible, so far as it depends on you, live peaceably with all." When we change our responses, we can affect others positively. I know who I would be without the influence and work of the Lord in my life. And there are people who have looked past who I was being at a certain time and said, "That's not all of her," as they challenged me live differently. A good God or friend does not excuse hurtful behavior but guides us to love with integrity. Like in the story with my children, Jesus shows us how to acknowledge our emotions without reciprocating them.

I told my mom after having my second child that I was praying for patience. She responded with a slight cringe, "Yikes! Be careful with that prayer!"

"Why?" I asked.

"Because the last time I prayed for that, I got you!"

Parenting requires great patience. You get these tiny humans and watch them grow from the ground up. You have them throughout their immature years, send them into adult life, and then patiently wait to see who they become. When my brother left for college, my mom cried. When I left, I'm pretty sure she clapped.

In Luke 15:11–32 (NKJV), Jesus gave us the parable of the prodigal son. A wealthy man had two sons. The younger came to him and asked for his inheritance, which they usually didn't get until the father passed away. But it says the father "divided to them his livelihood." Note that fact that is says "them" and not just "him," suggesting that the father gave the older son his portion as well, which he didn't even ask for. Also, culturally speaking, because he was the younger son, he got even less than the older one did. At that time, the younger son would typically receive about a third of the father's estate while the older son would get two-thirds. In essence, this son was saying to his father, "I wish you were dead, but you're not. Can I have my money and leave anyway?" Ouch! Can you imagine how used this father mut have felt? The son didn't want a relationship with his father and couldn't wait to distance himself from him.

Luke 15:13–19 (NKJV) says,

> Not many days after the younger son gathered all together, journeyed to a far country, and there wasted his possessions with prodigal living. But when he had spent all, there arose a severe famine in that land, and he began to be in want. The he went and joined himself to a citizen of that country, and he sent him into his fields to feed swine. And he would gladly have filled his stomach with the pods

that the swine ate, and no one gave him anything. But when he came to himself, he said "How many of my fathers hired servants have bread enough and to spare, and I perish with hunger!"

I originally thought that *prodigal* meant "rebellious," but it actually means "recklessly spendthrift." While the prodigal son behaved like this, we see that the father did as well. He gave his sons what they asked for, showered them with gifts, and gave generously to others. During this time, the son reflected on his father's character. His new employer was not as generous as his father had been. I like how it says, "My father's hired servants." They weren't slaves; they were paid and paid well as it said, "They had enough bread to spare."

It reminds me of when I left home. I couldn't wait to get out from underneath my parents and out of the small town I'd grown up in. However, it didn't take me long to miss all the things my parents had given me and had done for me. Being able to afford more than a PBJ was extravagant living for me in college. You wouldn't believe how many times $1 put into the vending machine bought me lunch. You can't always appreciate how fortunate you are until simple luxuries are taken away.

The story continues in Luke 15:18–24 (NKJV).

I will arise and go to my father, and will say to him, "father, I have sinned against heaven and before you, and I am no longer worthy to be called your son." And he arose and came to his father. But when he was still a great way off, his father saw him and had compassion and ran and fell on his neck and kissed him. And the son said to him, "Father I have sinned against heaven and in your sight, and am no longer worthy to be called your son." but the father said to his servants, "Bring out the best robe and put it on him, and put a ring on his hand and sandals on his feet. And bring the fatted calf here and kill it, and let us eat and be merry; for this my son was dead and is alive again; he was lost and is found." And they began to be merry.

Rock bottom is a powerful place, and the only way to get out is by acknowledging how you got there. The ladder out of the self-destruction pit is self-control, and the road to recovery is repentance. I love the part that says, "When he was still a great way off his father saw him." The father had never given up on him; he'd been watching and waiting patiently for him to come home. When he saw him coming, he ran to him with compassion in his heart. And then, he celebrated his return and lavishly poured out his love on him.

We can choose to walk away from someone who loves us. We no longer see the value or need in how they loved us, so we leave to find someone we think will be better. We stop wanting to wait for the good things God wants to give us, and we go out to get them on our own. Usually when we do that, we end up seeing that we've settled for less than the best. God has a plan for us, and He wants to give us His best. We don't live robotically under His control though, and we can choose to walk away from Him and His plans.

The older brother wasn't happy his brother was home and was mad about how his father reacted. He didn't think his younger brother deserved to be forgiven. He was the responsible one who had stayed. Pouting like a baby, he told his dad, "You never gave me a young goat that I might make merry with my friends." Really? He had gotten even more from his dad in the inheritance because he was the older son!

God Himself is a prodigal Father who spends His love extravagantly on His children from start to finish. Jesus taught this story in the presence of the Pharisees, the religious leaders at that time. He gave this illustration to them after being ridiculed for "receiving sinners and eating with them." They related to Jesus being more like them and wouldn't mind having Him in their group if He would agree to stop associating with outcasts. A good appearance was all that mattered to them.

Jesus came onto the scene and blew religion out of the water by teaching that relationships and the condition of the heart were what mattered the most. He showed it in His actions and with His teaching that none of us is better than another. Even if morally we've fallen "worse" than another in society's eyes, we haven't in God's.

In 1 Samuel 16:7 (NKJV), we read, "The Lord does not see as man sees; for man looks at the outward appearance but the Lord looks at the heart." We have a patient Father in heaven who is longing to see us come to Him even if we've just come from the pigpen and have nothing to show for the life He has given us. He wants to sit at our table and hear our stories, and He doesn't care what others think about that.

Jesus is the perfect example of how true love is patient no matter our behavior or condition. True love does not diminish based on the recipient's behavior or status but is patient in all circumstances.

CHAPTER 3

I MEAN I'M KIND

(Love is Kind)

Research shows that kindness improves our overall health by decreasing pain, stress, anxiety, depression, and blood pressure. Kindness produces oxytocin, called the love hormone. Oxytocin increases self-esteem and optimism, and like most medical antidepressants, kindness stimulates the production of serotonin. These chemicals light up our brains' pleasure and reward centers.

When we act in a kind way, the chemicals we need to be happy are produced organically. Doctors have found that the compassion muscle can be built up just as regular muscles can be, and its effects are contagious. When an act of kindness is performed, oxytocin is released in the brain and has the ability to be produced in the brains of bystanders as well.[1] Kindness and love are connected. When we are kind to someone, our brains produce the love hormone, and when we love someone, we are compelled to be kind to him or her.

One time, I was at a bridal shower for my cousin. I brought Thor, my son, who was four then. While we were there, a woman walked up to me limping and asked, "Is he your son?" while she looked at Thor, who was eating a cupcake.

"Yes he is," I replied.

"I just met him in the bathroom. Do you have a minute to talk?" she asked.

My mind started rattling off reasons she would want to talk to me about Thor. *Had he not shut the door? Had he crawled under the stall? Ugh, I should've gone with him, Why—*

She interrupted my thoughts. "I hope you don't mind, but I helped him wash his hands because he was having a hard time reaching the sink."

I felt my face getting red. "Oh no, I don't mind at all! Thank you for doing that. I'm sorry you had to help him. I should've known that and gone with him."

"Oh no! I was happy to help him. I wanted you to know that when I was washing his hands, he asked about mine." She extended her hands to me. I saw that her fingers were twisted, and I realized that her limp must have had something to do with that. She explained to me that ever since she was little, she had been crippled like that. She had told Thor the same thing. Her eyes began to well up with tears. She said, "Do you know what he said to me? He said that he thought they looked good. I kept on asking him if that's what he said because I thought maybe I'd heard him wrong. I usually don't get that response. Where do you think he got that?"

Tears began to well up in my eyes as I replied, "I don't know."

She smiled and said, "I think you do. I think you must have taught him that, and I want to thank you. I will carry this moment with me for the rest of my life."

I thought about how much kindness this woman must have had to show others when their comments weren't positive, how much she must have had to endure and yet how beautiful she was. I began to ask her who had taught her that, and Jesus was the answer to both of our question about one another's conduct. We both had given our lives to Christ and were trying to follow His example.

In John 8:2–11 (NKJV), Jesus showed us the kindness He gave to us and the kindness we should show others: "Now early in the morning He came again to the temple, and all the people came to Him; and He sat down and taught them." Jesus was someone people wanted to be around, and He didn't stand preaching at them … He sat and talked to them.

> Then the scribes and Pharisees brought to Him a woman caught in adultery. And when they had set her in the midst, they said to Him, "Teacher this woman was caught in adultery, in the very act. Now Moses, in the law commanded us that such should be stoned. But what do you say?"

Not just the woman should have been there according to the Mosaic law; both parties would be subject to this trial, which makes this feel even more like a setup. This woman was most likely a prostitute, and adultery was her means of living.

> This they said, testing Him, that they might have something of which to accuse Him. But Jesus

stooped down and wrote on the ground with His finger, as though He did not hear. So when they continued asking Him, He raised Himself up and said to them, "He who is without sin among you, let him throw a stone at her first." And again He stooped down and wrote on the ground. Then those who heard it, being convicted by their conscience, went out one by one, beginning with the oldest even to the last. And Jesus was left alone, and the women standing in the midst. When Jesus had raised Himself up and saw no one but the women and said to her, "Women, where are those accusers of yours? Has no one condemned you?" She said "No one, Lord" And Jesus said to her "Neither do I condemn you; go and sin no more." Then Jesus said to them "I am the light of the world. He who follows me shall not walk in darkness, but have the light of life."

All right, there's a lot more here than meets the eye. First of all, why does it say they were trying to test Jesus? Why would this be a test for Jesus? Roman law said that a person could be put to death only by a ruling of a judge. If Jesus would've told them to stone the woman, it would've gone against His sense of mercy, grace, and forgiveness. He would have also failed to be submitting to Roman authority. And if Jesus would have told the scribes and Pharisees to let her go, He wouldn't have been upholding Jewish law. So instead, He pricked their consciences by having them examine themselves, and they left convicted, but I'm not sure if they were convinced.

Sometimes, that's how we react to Jesus Christ as well. We feel like we've never heard God talk to us sometimes as humans, but when He pricks our consciences by showing us our sin and weaknesses, we turn away because that's not what we wanted to hear. Many times through our encounters with Jesus, we leave convicted but unconvinced and go back to the hurt God is trying to free us from. God's kindness speaks to us through our moral nature not to shame us but to show us.

The next picture we see is beautiful. As this half-naked woman stood there in shame, Jesus covered her in kindness and told her that He did not condemn her either. He didn't say that because He sinned as well; He said it because He knew her humanity. And when He told her to "go and sin no more," He wasn't asking her to be perfect; He was telling her to not go back to her former life because the life she was leading was dangerous and that the next time, He might not be there to save her from her accusers. Then He gave us the answer to how we can live life to the fullest—by following His light.

The apostle Paul wrote thirteen books of the Bible, mostly from a prison cell, but before he gave his life to Christ and began walking in the light, he was a religious zealot with a dark past and went by the name Saul.

Paul was of Jewish decent but a Roman citizen and was trained as a Pharisee. He worked his way up and had become a part of the Roman Sanhedrin. The Sanhedrin was recognized by the Romans as the political leader of the Jews; its members were at Jesus's trials, and after Jesus's death, they executed many Christians who believed Jesus was Christ, the Son of God, and those who spoke of seeing His risen body. Paul thought He was doing the right thing and protecting the Jewish religion, but His heart wasn't showing the love or kindness of Christ.[2]

In Acts 9 is the story of Paul's miraculous conversion to Christianity. One day on the road to Damascus, Paul (Saul) left the city into which he had gone to get letters giving him authority to bring Christians to Jerusalem in chains. Paul encountered Jesus for the first time through a light that shined around him from heaven and a voice asking him (Acts 9:4–5 NKJV), "Why are you persecuting me?"

Paul answered, "Who are you?"

The voice replied, "I am Jesus, whom you are persecuting."

Paul asked what he should do and was given instructions. Those with Paul heard the voice but saw no one. When Paul opened his eyes after the encounter, he couldn't see. But when he followed through with what the voice had told him to do, he regained his sight and was filled with the Holy Spirit.

In Titus 3:1–8 (NKJV), Paul wrote to a young pastor, Titus,

> Remind them to be subjected to rulers and authorities, to obey, to be ready for every good work, to speak evil of no one, to be peaceable, gentle, showing all humility to all men. For we ourselves were also once foolish, disobedient, deceived, serving various lusts and pleasures, living in malice and envy, hateful and hating one another. But when the kindness and love of God our Savior toward man appeared, not by works of righteousness which we have done, but according to His mercy He saved us through the washing of regeneration and renewing of the Holy Spirit whom He poured out on us abundantly through Jesus Christ our Savior, that having been justified

by His grace we should become heirs according to the hope of eternal life. This is a faithful saying and these things I want you to affirm constantly, that those who have believed in God should be careful to maintain good works. These things are profitable and good to men.

This passage is so significant because here you have Paul, a former religious zealot, admitting that before his conversion, he had been a sinner and yet to be in his position as a part of the Sanhedrin, he wasn't supposed to sin. His faith before was reliant on good works, but he was then telling a different story. He was saying in essence, "I know who I am, and I remember what I was. It was the kindness and love of God that changed me. I'm not justified because of what I've done but because of who God is."

Throughout these stories, we see how Jesus can change a mind and a heart and produce in us the outflow of kind action. God's kindness to humanity was shown on the cross through Jesus, and just like in the story of the adulterous woman, even when society condemns us, that isn't His purpose.

While God loves everyone, not everyone accepts His love. John 3:16–18 (NIV) reads,

For God so loved the world that He gave His one and only Son, that whoever believes in Him should not perish but have eternal life. For God did not send His Son into the world to condemn the world, but to save the world through Him. Whoever believes in Him is not condemned, but whoever does not believe stands condemned already, because

they have not believed in the name of God's one
and only Son.

It was kind for Jesus to say this; He was warning us of the danger of unbelief just as He warned the adulterous woman of the danger in the life she lived. Paul reminded us of the goodness that came from living in a Christlike way and showing others the kindness we receive from Jesus even when we are undeserving of it. Kindness is good and good for us; that's why God shows it to us and wants us to replicate it.

CHAPTER 4

MY HEART BLEEDS RED, BUT MY EYES SEE GREEN

(Love Does Not Envy)

E nvy always takes more than it can give; it doesn't just want. It wants to destroy. Hannah Segal said that envy "aims at spoiling the goodness of the object, to remove the source of envious feelings ... since a spoiled object arouses no envy."[1]

Psychology has deemed envy one of the darkest human emotions. An envious person admires an attribute and will go to great lengths to have it or have power over it. It's one of the top character traits of a narcissist, and at envy's very core, love is compromised. A person dominated by this emotion experiences enjoyment only when stealing another's joy.

I heard a story once that gave me a mental picture to link with this toxic quality. Two men shared a hospital room. Both were extremely ill and confined to their beds. The man closer to the window would spend day after day gazing out and painting verbal pictures of it for the man who couldn't see what was going on outside the window. He would tell him of kids playing, dogs running, lovers strolling, and weather turning. The man without the window view loved the stories; they brought much joy and adventure to his day.

One day while watching the man looking out the window, his mind began to turn. He thought of how unfair it was that the other man got to be by the window. He longed to have this man's spot. He felt that his life would be so much better if he got to see all the scenes unfolding firsthand. The man by the window seemed so happy, and the man without the window wanted that happiness.

One day while eating lunch, the man by the window began to choke. He looked at the man next to him in desperation. The man knew he should call for help, but he really wanted his spot in the room. So as the man by the window continued to choke, he rolled over in bed pretending not to see and closed his eyes as if he were asleep.

In that moment, his jealousy turned to envy. When the nurses came in, they were distraught, and the man said, "I don't know what happened. He was fine earlier today," knowing full well he could have cried out on this man's behalf and they could've saved him. However, there was the thrilling thought of getting what he wanted, and so his remorse subsided. He couldn't wait to have that view. He dreamed about it all night.

The next day, he was moved to the window spot and was thrilled with anticipation. He closed his eyes eager to feel the sun on his face as the nurse drew back the curtain. When he opened his eyes, his heart sank in disappointment. The only thing he could see was the side of another building. He realized that all that time, the other man had been making up those stories to entertain him. He had killed the very source of his joy the day before when he let envy determine his choice.

You can't have something others possess by taking it from them. You can try to steal their joy, but you can't hold onto it. Envy never lives up to its promise because it's not trying to take an object. Even if you envy a possession such as a bigger house or a new toy, what you are really longing for is the feeling you think that possession will give you. It's grasping for a characteristic. Even though logically you know you can't have it, you may settle for the next best thing and set out to destroy it.

Most toxic people put themselves or their possessions on pedestals and tear down everything else around them. Picture rock climbers in a competition to get to the top. They start out even, but then someone starts to pull away and get ahead. It makes the ones behind feel inferior, and they hadn't entered the competition to lose. Climbers start grabbing the heels of anyone who passes them by to propel themselves farther up. That is envy. Instead of just staying your course and doing the best you can win or lose, you decide to take others out. In real life, this can mean vandalizing property or slandering, bullying, or blackmailing others.

This envy plant leaves us hungering. We can misplace our affections and go after things that leave us only salivating for more. Gratitude is the course that ends this type of starvation.

In 1 Kings 3:16–28 (NKJV), King Solomon gave us a way to test our hearts and motives. In this story were two prostitutes who had given birth three days apart. During the night, one of the prostitutes rolled over on her baby and killed it. She then switched the dead baby with the other's live baby and in the morning was accused of doing so.

During this battle of "she said, she said," Solomon declared that the live baby would be cut in half. One woman cried out, "O my lord, give her the living child, and by no means kill him!" while the other woman said, "Let him be neither mine nor yours, but divide him." Solomon said, "Give the first woman the living child, and by no means kill him; she is the mother."

It's sad that we can at times rationalize our grief with a shrug, throw up our hands, and say, "It's not fair. I should be happy. If I'm not, no one else should be. I don't care about the good things I have. I want the good things they have."

We get this grass-is-greener mentality because the lens we're looking through has become green with envy. When we take off the filter and observe, we see with clarity that our grass, even if it's not the same color, has the same potential. There's poop over on their side of the fence too, and they have gone just as many days without rain. But if we aren't watering our lawn or turning those feces into fertilizer, we will just be walking around on our brown grass and getting poop stuck to the bottom of our shoes.

We all to some extent inherited pieces of life that resemble less-than-desirable lawns, situations we had no control over. Worldwide, we've experienced the dusty deserts of the coronavirus pandemic. We get all turned around in a dry place where every day, the sand is blowing at us from a different direction and no one has a compass.

Maybe you were born with a disability, unstable home life, low income, or debilitating anxiety or depression. I don't know what your affliction is, but you're not alone; someone out there has a similar story. Others were born with what the world sees as brown grass too; they're just not willing to let that be how it stays. When we give those places over to God, He can cultivate and care for them. Our outside circumstances may or may not change, but our hearts can be transformed even amid trials. God wants to throw out the world's green-tinted filter that shows you all this life has to offer is material and give you the eyes that see eternal potential.

Jeremiah 29:11(NIV) reads, "'For I know the plans I have for you,' declares the LORD, 'plans to prosper you and not harm you, plans to give you hope and a future.'" Those plans, that prosperity, does not happen internally unless the soil is drenched in the loving-kindness of our Lord and Savior, Jesus Christ. His Word, the Bible, gives us wisdom; it searches our hearts and extracts the true intent of our actions. God declares divided the coveted object and justly rules seeing the intent of our hearts.

No matter what terrain we have been set in, we can choose what we do with it. God allows us to exist there not to be cruel but to show us how He can turn a disappointing desert into a garden of gratitude.

CHAPTER 5

HELP! I'VE FALLEN AND I CAN'T GET UP

(Love Does Not Boast)

There is a difference between pride and confidence, and confidence can be a great thing. Growing up, I wasn't very athletic, but I liked sports. My parents allowed my brother and me to be in one spring sport starting in seventh grade. I walked onto the softball team pretty raw and spent most of my time on the bench. In tenth grade, I tried my hand at track because I was told I had a runner's body. News flash—Having a runner's body doesn't mean you can run. I failed at that too.

In eleventh grade, I switched back to softball, and much to my surprise, I made varsity. During practice, I really felt I was starting to gain control over my gangly body, and new glasses helped my depth perception immensely.

Our first home game, I took my place as a starter in left field.

I turned around to see a truck full of every guy I ever had a crush on watching from the fence. I was literally shaking. The third play of the game was a pop fly right to me. I ran up on it but misjudged and had to backpedal. I tripped, and the ball fell behind me. I sat there in disappointment as the center fielder ran over to get the ball. After that, I was—You guessed it—back on the bench. I felt awful. I had disappointed my team and made a fool of myself.

A few games after that, a fielder failed to catch three balls but our coach didn't pull her. I didn't get it. *Why does he keep her out there after three mistakes but pulls me off after one mistake?* I wondered. It was as if my coach had read my mind. After the game, he talked about how mistakes would happen but that we were not to let that shake our confidence. When we fail, how we recover is the most important consideration. It clicked for me with that statement. It wasn't that I had messed up; it was that I had sat in my failure and had let someone else pick up the pieces.

For the next few games, I sat on the bench and cheered as loud and as hard as I could. I was going to make my mark on the team in whatever position I was in. After my senior year, I won the Most Improved Player award, but it had taken failure to earn it.

The Samaritan woman in this next story had dropped a few balls in the game of life. She knew what it felt like to fail, and she desired to be loved, accepted, and forgiven. On the bench of life, she got the privilege of becoming Jesus's water boy. What He gave her in return was a spot on His team. I would even dare say that she went on to win a reward similar to mine from her new coach.

John 4:6–29 (NIV) reads,

> Jacob's well was there, and Jesus, tired as he was
> from the journey, sat down by the well. It was about

noon. When a Samaritan woman came to draw water, Jesus said to her, "Will you give me a drink?" (His disciples had gone into the town to buy food.) The Samaritan woman said to him, "You are a Jew and I am a Samaritan woman. How can you ask me for a drink?" (For Jews do not associate with Samaritans.) Jesus answered her, "If you knew the gift of God and who it is that asks you for a drink, you would have asked him and he would have given you living water."

"Sir," the woman said, "you have nothing to draw with and the well is deep. Where can you get this living water? Are you greater than our father Jacob, who gave us the well and drank from it himself, as did also his sons and his livestock?"

Jesus answered, "Everyone who drinks this water will be thirsty again, but whoever drinks the water I give them will never thirst. Indeed, the water I give them will become in them a spring of water welling up to eternal life." The woman said to him, "Sir, give me this water so that I won't get thirsty and have to keep coming here to draw water."

He told her, "Go, call your husband and come back." "I have no husband," she replied. Jesus said to her, "You are right when you say you have no husband. The fact is, you have had five husbands, and the man you now have is not your husband. What you have just said is quite true."

"Sir," the woman said, "I can see that you are a prophet. Our ancestors worshiped on this mountain, but you Jews claim that the place where we must worship is in Jerusalem."

"Woman," Jesus replied, "believe me, a time is coming when you will worship the Father neither on this mountain nor in Jerusalem. You Samaritans worship what you do not know; we worship what we do know, for salvation is from the Jews. Yet a time is coming and has now come when the true worshipers will worship the Father in the Spirit and in truth, for they are the kind of worshipers the Father seeks. God is spirit, and his worshipers must worship in the Spirit and in truth."

The woman said, "I know that Messiah" (called Christ) "is coming. When he comes, he will explain everything to us."

Then Jesus declared, "I, the one speaking to you—I am he."

John 4:39–42 (NIV) reads,

Many of the Samaritans from that town believed in him because of the woman's testimony, "He told me everything I ever did." So when the Samaritans came to him, they urged him to stay with them, and he stayed two days. And because of His words many more became believers. They said to the woman, "We no longer believe just because of what you said; now we have heard for ourselves, and we know that this man really is the Savior of the world."

Jesus sat down to have an honest conversation with a broken woman. She had been married five times and was living with a man she was not married to. She makes me smile. She is honest and blunt, and Jesus wasn't offended by her or her questions. Jesus and this woman had little common ground before this conversation. He was male, and she was a female. He was a Jew, and she was a Samaritan. They had different religious beliefs, but they spoke candidly and had a meaningful conversation.

Jesus saw her fully and did not condemn her but spoke love into her life. He did not treat her or her people as outcasts or less-thans. He stayed with them and talked to them. And in the end, others did not believe just because of what the woman told them but because they had conversed with Jesus. This to me shows the importance of seeking a personal relationship with Christ, not just going off what other people tell you about Him. It's important for you to have your own journey of faith.

My grandfather Paul and my husband's grandfather Wally had a relationship that testifies to my point. They were best friends, good ol' boys from the middle of nowhere who bonded over their love for horses and drinking. Paul and Wally used to frequent a bar where legend had it that Paul would run his mouth and Wally would smash in faces. On the way back home, they'd share a bottle and Wally would make a game out of getting Paul to laugh so hard that he'd fall off his horse.

These rebels ran their lives throwing caution to the wind until one day, God came knocking on Wally's heart. Wally's wife had given her life to the Lord, and after seeing the change in her, he decided to make the same commitment. When Wally presented the message to Paul, he rejected it. It wasn't until months later while noticing the change in Wally that he decided he wanted that for his life as well. They started a church together with their families, and that church is the one I attend today with my husband.

People shouldn't just believe in Jesus and His love because of my testimony or my family story, but they should be able to see a difference in our lives. Maybe you will decide you want a relationship like that with God, or maybe not. But part of the reason Jesus needed to exist on earth was to connect the unseen and seen worlds. His purposes convict the heart, cause repentance, and redeem our souls for God's glory. When Jesus enters someone's life, He changes it. That change affects the person's family, and that family can change a community. A relationship with God takes a humble heart; even Jesus submitted to the will of His Father.

Philippians 2:5–8 (NKJV) reads,

> Let this mind be in you which was also in Christ Jesus, who, being in the form of God did not consider it robbery to be made equal with God but made Himself of no reputation, taking the form of a bondservant, and coming in the likeness of men. And being found in appearance as a man, He humbled Himself and became obedient to the point of death, even the death of the cross.

David Jeremiah wrote a footnote on 2:7 (NKJV).

> Jesus sacrificed none of His deity, yet came in perfect humility (the form of a bondservant) by taking on flesh and becoming fully man. By this, He voluntarily submitted Himself to the authority of God the Father and the empowerment of the

Holy Spirit. He also confined Himself to a human body. Likeness suggests similarity but difference. Jesus humanity was genuine, but he differed from other humans in that He was sinless (Romans 8:3 NKJV; Hebrews 4:15 NKJV) and in full possession of another nature-God's.[1]

Jesus humbled Himself and sacrificed the comfort and love He had in heaven to come to earth. His obedience was a representation of the love He had for His Father and their love for humanity. I have failed royally at times to be obedient to God's commands. Failing doesn't mean you're a failure though. When Jesus came in humility, He made a way for the fallen to be lifted up. He made a way for the broken to be healed. He made a way for those searching for love to find it.

Whom are you playing for? Whose team are you on? If it's God's team, you will always have a place, and when you are faithful with the little tasks, He will give you bigger ones. Your attitude on the bench is the one you carry onto the field. Cultivate humility in your humanity and confidence in God's deity. Pursue the goal of improving regardless of your current position.

CHAPTER 6

FEELING BLOATED? IT'S YOUR SALTY SELF

(Love Does Not Dishonor)

I mentioned the word *narcissistic* in the chapter on envy, but let me dive in deeper here. Narcissistic personality disorder, NPD, is defined as "a disorder in which a person has an inflated sense of self-importance." Its very definition means to be "puffed up."[1]

The disorder is found more commonly in men but is rare; less than 1 percent of the world has been diagnosed with this condition. Yet it is said that everyone has moments of this behavior even if their lives is not characterized by it. Symptoms of this disorder as defined by the Mayo Clinic include, "an excess need for admiration, disregard for other's feelings, and inability to handle any criticism, and a sense of entitlement."[2] Also, for my hypochondriac friends, if you think you might be a narcissist, you most likely are not. Part of NPD is a lack of self-awareness; if you were one, you would not see yourself that way.

There are hundreds of examples of NPD throughout history, and some would say it is more prevalent now than ever. The example I'll look at is Adolf Hitler. When you look at his life's journey, it is hard to understand how he, a mediocre artist, rose to become the dictator of Germany. I think his life is important to look at when we are dealing with choices on how to live and love. On the scale of humanity's darkness, Hitler's case is extreme, but sometimes, contrast is the tool we need to find depth and pick up on detail.

Hitler's early childhood was plagued with rejection. His father beat him, and he was not well liked in school. He did however seem to have a loving mother whom he lost in 1908. In 1907, he failed to get into art school, and by 1909, he was homeless. In 1913, he joined the German army, and during his service in World War I, he seemed to find a place in the world.

Soon, he found himself working with the military information unit and was introduced to the German Workers' Party. In 1919, during a party lecture, Hitler argued about an idea. The leader of the party liked Hitler's speaking style so much that he asked him to become its fifty-fifth member. In 1921, he became chairmen under the foundation's new name, the National Socialist German Workers, or Nazi for short.

When Germany lost World War I, the German people were shocked. They had been told that they had been winning the war. The shock did not bring just devastation though. Conspiracy theories began to pop up, and because of people's willingness to pass the blame, Jewish people were being held accountable. From the viewpoint of Hitler and the Nazi regime, Jews were the reason they lost the war. They said that Jews had become traitors and that they needed to be exterminated. Hitler became obsessed with the idea of ethnic "purity" and ranked the Aryan race as he called it at the top.

In 1932, Hitler ran for president. To push off the negative press, his team polished his public image and blanketed his private life. They presented him as a morally upright man with a private life to prove it. When you look closely at his private life, you see anything but that description. But hey, that's politics, right?

Hitler slowly began to seduce the German people by presenting himself as a dog-loving, child-kissing gentlemen. The media sold the image, and people ate it up. Germans were coming off a severe low, and they needed something or someone to believe in. They began to believe that Hitler could fix it all, and with media's help, he became a celebrity.

Nazis attained only 37 percent of the vote during the 1932 election, but by the next year, the tide was turning. In February 1933, Germany's parliament building was set on fire and a Dutch Communist was accused of the crime. Later evidence suggested that the Nazi regime was to blame. That was the straw that Hitler used to break the camel's back. On March 23, the parliament turned over full control to Hitler and his Nazi soldiers. [2]

By 1935, the Nuremberg Laws deprived Jews of German citizenship and banned them from having relationships or marrying "German blood." Year after year, they took more and more away from the Jews at the same time World War II began to break out, and Hitler's army began to form alliances. As the Gestapo killed and detained Jews in Germany, the Nazi army went to the front lines. They were fighting a war outside their country and inside.

After war broke out, the Nazis shifted from sending Jews to controlled territories to killing them. Jewish people were the target, but gypsies, Catholics, homosexuals, the disabled, and political dissidents were killed too. Some were used for science experiments under the hand of Joseph Mengele, and some were forced into labor. Most Jews were killed in gas chambers. By the end of the German war, some 6 million humans had been exterminated.

Hitler had succeeded in transforming Germany and the European world. On April 30 of 1945, he shot himself, but his impact still burns.[3] It has been said that Hitler's reign was the closest humans have ever come to seeing what a world would look like without God. During his time, hate took control and humans had become the deciding factor of others' value and fate. Love for self at the expense of others' lives was deemed acceptable. There have been many things done in history including the oppression of races that we cannot undo. At every point in history when humans began to rate themselves against other humans, demoralization came with it. We may have left the caste system, but remnants are still found in the veins of humanity. Every day, social media greets us with the disheartened ideologies of comparison.

Hitler came from a very lonely place. He had just lost his mother; rejection was his middle name. He then found himself in a position where he was liked and the people around him were seemingly on his team. People helped him rise to his position. They offered him adoration, power, position, fame, money, and a place in history. They did not only accept his hate and aggression; they also fueled it. He did not kill 6 million people alone, and the people and voices we allow to speak to us can lead us down destructive paths instead of pulling us off them.

If I weren't a Christian and someone offered me fame, fortune, and position at the expense of my integrity, I'd take it. I, however, believe that my identity is found in Jesus Christ and that His ideologies are for my good and the good of others. That is why I try living the way I do. If I didn't have that, I would inflate myself, selfishly seduce others, and not care whom I was hurting in the process as long as I was getting what I wanted. Hitler and I naturally at the core are not so different. Our flesh wants the same things, but the way we think morally is on opposing spectrums.

What do you gain by living only for yourself and selfish motives? You may get what you want, but what will you lose in the process? In her book *Uninvited*, Lisa TerKeurst wrote, "The mind feasts on what it focuses on. What consumes my thinking will be the making or the breaking of my identity."[4] What do you find your identity in? Mark 8:36 (NIV) says, "For what does it profit a man to gain the whole world, yet forfeit his soul?"

What you believe about life, yourself, and others is the foundation on which you build your morality. Yes, you were influenced by your parents, and as you grew older, you held onto their influence but pick up other influences. I questioned what my parents had taught me. It was important for me to do so in order to grow and develop in my faith. It was also important for me to recognize the value and love they gave me because of their faith. Their belief wasn't just spoken but lived out not perfectly but clearly. Matthew 7:24–27 (NLT) puts it like this.

> Anyone who listens to my teachings and follows it is wise, like a person who builds a house on a solid rock. Though the rain comes in torrents and the floodwaters rise and the winds beat against that house, it will not collapse because it is built on a bedrock. But anyone who hears my teaching and does not obey it is foolish, like a person who

builds a house on sand. When the rains and floods come and the winds beat against that house, it will collapse with a mighty crash.

Our lives represent our way of thinking, but we can't look only at outward actions or appearances. Good home inspectors don't look only at a house's appearance; they are not fooled by beautiful landscaping and curb appeal. They will make sure the structure and foundation are good.

We can look at someone's life without seeing the structural damage below the surface. We should be careful about whom we let influence us and check our motivations when we step into someone else's. Jeremiah 17:9–10 (NIV) says,

> The heart is deceitful above all things and beyond cure. Who can understand it? Who can see the unseen things in our hearts and lives? I the Lord search the heart and examine the mind, to reward each person according to their conduct, according to what their deeds deserve.

My parents gave me a good foundation on which to build my life, but when I was an adult, I didn't live in the house they had built. I went out on my own. God knows every crack in my foundation. He sees all my painful moments. That is why He is the perfect engineer for building my life. Just like the end of the verse states though, if I don't hire Him, the damage is on me.

Love is humble. It grounds itself in truth, not selfish motivations and dictatorship. Love says, I know what's best for you, but you have to make your own decisions. I will not force you to live my way. I will present to you the best option and a way out, but I cannot save you from the consequences of walking on the path you choose to take.

What we choose to believe matters not only to us; it also matters to others. The value of life exists because God gave it significance when He created it. I am not above anyone else, and if my life doesn't exemplify that, love isn't being seen.

David Jeremiah wrote, "The greatest moral force in the world is not the law but love. Love for God and for others empowers people to do what they cannot accomplish in the flesh-fulfill the law."[5] One of the greatest ways to show love is through humility and regard for others.

CHAPTER 7

I LOVE YOU, BUT I LIKE ME MORE

(Love Is Not Self-Seeking)

t's the first snowfall of the year. My children bounce out of bed at the ever-loving hour of 6:30 a.m. to start digging out every piece of snow gear in preparation for their adventure. These are the same children who usually do not function until their caloric intake has regulated their hangry little attitudes.

My youngest is famous for stumbling out of his bedroom half-asleep and informing anyone who will listen that he is hungry. He will not rest his case no matter how chaotic the morning may be until someone delivers on his demands. The persistence and pure desperation in his voice would leave you thinking that he had not eaten for days. Today, though, we have turned over new leaves, and apparently, a snowflake is the breakfast of champions.

I on the other hand could not be less thrilled about the dandruff falling from the sky. I do not want to jump out of bed. I would rather pull the sheets over my head and dream about summer, sun, and sand. Why in the world I live in northern Minnesota when I hate the cold is a mystery to everyone and his or her mother.

As I help the kids get dressed and scrounge up enough materials to cover their adorable little phalanges, their excitement and joy starts affecting me. As they pile out the door, I look out the window. My youngest is feeding the dog snow out of one hand and shoveling some in for himself with the other. I see them laughing, smiling, and playing, and all of a sudden I realize I am smiling too. Emotionally, I have done a 180. Their happiness is bringing me joy. Your girl is feelin' them vibes. (This sentence right here btw is how I actually talk, and this book is proof that God works miracles.)

Imagine if I would have pushed my feelings on them. We sometimes do that to their little hearts. I could have told them that they were not going outside and convinced them that there was nothing good about this snow situation.

We may be adults, but that doesn't mean we're always right. My kids have taught me more than I could have ever imagined. Sometimes, our jaded adult minds construe happiness and focus on the objective instead of the subjective. The objective facts of this situation are that this day marks the beginning of a six-month period in which white flakes are the primary scenery and warm layers are a necessity. The subjective though is that my kids love this season even if I don't. Why should I stand in the way of that? It is not harming them to take joy from and to see the beauty in this season; it's helping them.

We are emotional and intelligent beings who are given reason and choice. I think if we evaluate situations devoid of facts and look only at emotion, our conclusions become half-truths. The same is true if we rely solely on emotions and throw out facts. The truth about winter is that it's long and cold up here in the north but that moments of joy and pleasure come with it as well.

I love watching my children exercise their freedom to make healthy choices such as enjoying the snow. As a parent, I am here to guide, direct, and protect them. I'll warn them of course about danger in destructive choices; I wouldn't be a very good guide if I didn't. I know that they will make mistakes just as I have and that they will learn from them as I have. Discernment is key; don't pick a fight over opinions. When your child becomes an adult and dyes his or her hair purple, your greatest concern should still be what's going on in his or her heart.

If God is a good and loving Father, the commands He gives will reflect His character and be for our benefit. Power-hungry dictators give rules based on their personal opinions and preferences. They want everyone to value what they value; those who don't fit the mold get tossed aside.

So what do God's commands tell us about Him? Are they for our good? Let's look at the Ten Commandments (Exodus 20:2–17 NIV).

1. You shall have no other gods before me.
2. You shall not make idols.
3. You shall not take the name of the Lord your God in vain.
4. Remember the Sabbath day, to keep it holy.
5. Honor your father and mother.
6. You shall not murder.
7. You shall not commit adultery.
8. You shall not steal.
9. You shall not bear false witness against your neighbor.
10. You shall not covet.

The first commandment seems a bit self-centered, doesn't it? But if we were made by God and He is the source of life, wouldn't it be in our best interests to plug into this source? If we are aligning our will with our Creator's will, life is not only more coherent; it is also more joy filled. It gives us a sense of what Adam and Eve must have experienced before sin entered the world.

Let's look at number two—no idols. If God is the real thing, anything else that presents itself as God is fake. Eventually, counterfeit gods will fail to do what God can; to detect false gods, we must know the true God first. Bank tellers study real money so that when fake bills present themselves, they can spot them.

What does it mean to take the Lord's name in vain? Another word for vain is emptiness. We are not to take the Lord's name and claim it is empty; it has value.

Remember that the Sabbath is holy. This was important because even God rested and reflected after creating the world. Rest and reflection allow for perception. Jesus was accused of breaking this law in Matthew 12:10–14, Mark 3:2–6, and John 9:14–16 when He healed a man on the Sabbath. When you read the accounts, you see that he was not disregarding the Sabbath; rather, He was showing the Pharisees how legalistic they had become. They were twisting the intent of the law, which in turn violated the law (Matthew 15:9; Mark 7:1–13; John 7:19; Galatians 6:13). The Pharisees had added to this law a bunch of unneeded and cumbersome by-laws.

We have to be careful as churchgoers not to become legalistic. Rituals can disengage the heart and become robotic. God is more interested in a relationship that changes the heart than a religion that changes actions. You can do everything right in religion's eyes and have a heart that is far from God. We see this happen in marriages all the time; marriages can die and becomes more like business transactions, two people just going through the motions. God wants to have intentional relationships with us. The Sabbath is to be a day of rest and reflection on God's goodness and holiness; we are to check our hearts and ask for forgiveness for the ways we have hurt that relationship. It was meant to be an intimate time. I don't go to church on Sunday because I have to or because I think it'll get me to heaven. I go because it does me good, puts life back into perspective, and helps me evaluate my heart.

Honor you father and mother. Imperfect people raising imperfect people can be a bit of a disaster at times. This one boggled my mind for a bit because some parents just don't seem to be deserving of honor. It made me think of the movie *I Can Only Imagine*. If you haven't seen it, give it a watch. It tells the true story of Bart Millard. Bart's dad in the movie had a drinking problem and beat him severely all throughout his childhood. In real life, his dad did horrifically beat him. He didn't have a drinking problem but a serious anger issue. Bart hated his dad for the things he had to endure, but then his dad gave his heart to Christ and things changed. Bart said, "I grew up thinking that if the gospel could change that guy, it could change anyone. There was no denying it." Honoring our parents can be a testimony to them. Bart forgave his dad and worked on a relationship with him. The change in his son's life led him to change his life.

Remember the order of the commandments. God is true and comes first. Idols are false and will lack. Rest and reflect one day a week to make sure to check your heart's position, and ask for forgiveness when you fail in the relationship. Then honor your father and mother; listen to and respect them because Israel had seen firsthand how God had delivered them from slavery in Egypt.

Our sin has a way of capturing and enslaving us, but God wants to set us free. When we are honest about how our sin and rebellion against God negatively impact our lives, we give our children tangible evidence and reasons to listen to Him and His guidance. In Ephesians 6:2 (NIV), this commandment comes with a promise "so that it may go well with you and that you may enjoy a long life on earth." When our parents are living godly lives and tell us about how God delivered them from a life of captivity, God says listen to that, respect it. If you do, things will go better for you and you will enjoy life more.

We are going to clump these last ones together because they all speak of keeping our integrity. Integrity is the quality of being honest and having strong moral principles. This is the part of the Ten Commandments where we see God's transcendent morality was given to humans as well. He does care about how we live; He says we are not to murder, cheat, steal, lie, or covet. Some translations will say "kill," but the Hebrew word used here is *ratzah*, "murder." Murder involves unlawful premeditation, not self-defense … a huge difference. Big shout-out to the police and soldiers who uphold that and protect and defend others and themselves lawfully; I appreciate them and their sacrifices.

If I am being a good parent, I do not press my personal preferences on my children and make them feel ashamed if they think differently. I do not want them to hurt others or get hurt, so I guide them on paths that I hope will prevent that. I explained before about my feelings toward snow; their believing different from me in that area was good for them and me.

When I tell my kids to look both ways before crossing the road, I do so to make them aware of the possibility of being struck by a car if they don't look both ways. I don't want my kids to be afraid of crossing the street, but I want them to understand the possible danger so they can proceed with awareness. The God of the Bible is that same kind of parent; He doesn't selfishly make rules to infringe on our rights; He knows that our following Him will lead to our greatest freedom. John 8:36 (ESV) reads, "So if the Son sets you free, you will be free indeed."

Hindsight can be twenty-twenty; like a loving parent, God tries to keep us away from ideologies and life paths that will hurt us and others. As parents, we want our children take us at our word and not have to see by experiencing something dangerous. Sometimes, they don't listen, and we're forced to let go of the reins and let them make mistakes. If we can save them from the hurt in the first place by directing them though, why wouldn't we?

An unseen moral God knows what things we should stay away from because He sees what we can't. Without a moral law, we would be children running around with knives in our hands with no parents to explain the dangers inherent in that.

God gave us the commandments because He knows our human properties; He sees through their cosmetic display and knows us at our core. He gives them to us for our protection and for our good. He gives them to us because He loves us.

CHAPTER 8

I FIGHT LIKE A GIRL

(Love Is Not Easily Angered)

When we were growing up, my brother and I would get into fights. When it came to wrestling matches, because he was a boy and two years older than me, I had to fight dirty just to hold my own. Bite, scratch, pull hair, pinch, slap, and I still got outmatched.

But as I grew up, I learned that if I mentally messed with him, I'd gain the upper hand. Blackmail became a great ally. If I could do something quietly to make him lose his temper while my parents were in sight, his reaction would be their focus.

Is that who the God of the Bible is? Putting up roadblocks, knowing we are going to fail, and ready to strike when we do? How could a loving God put the tree of temptation in the garden? Was God provoking us by conducting this social experiment? If He is all knowing, He knew that humans would fail, so why then make us at all? Just for His own pleasure?

I know this is a lot to unpack, but I also feel they are good questions to ask. Let's look at the story first and then dive into those deep questions.

Genesis 3:1 (NKJV) reads,

> Now the serpent was more cunning that any beast of the field which the Lord God had made. And he said to the women, "Has God indeed said, 'You shall not eat of every tree of the Garden'?"

Satan loves to feed us questions that make us doubt what God has really said.

Genesis 3:2–3 (NKJV) reads,

> And the woman said to the serpent, "We may eat the fruit of the trees of the garden; but of the fruit of the tree which is in the midst of the garden, God has said, 'You shall not eat it, nor shall you touch it, lest you die.'"

Right here, we recognize that Eve knew what God had said to her but was on her way to denying it.

Genesis 3:4 (NKJV) reads,

> Then the serpent said to the woman, "You will not surely die. For God knew that in the day that you eat of it your eyes will be opened, and you will be like God, knowing good and evil."

The serpent accused God of being jealous. Have you ever thought that God was cruel by not letting you experience everything? Why does God give us a moral code to live by? If God does not want us to do something, why would He give us the desire to do it?

Genesis 3:5 (NKJV) tells us,

> So when the woman saw that the tree was good for food, that it was pleasant to the eyes, and a tree desirable to make one wise, she took of its fruit and ate. She also gave to her husband and he ate. Then the eyes of both of them were opened, and they knew that they were naked; and they sewed fig leaves together and made themselves coverings.

Satan had gotten Adam and Eve to believe that God was not good and did not have their best interests in mind. In doing this, he got them to throw out God's will and instead obey their own desires.

Eve reached out for things she already had—the beautiful garden and a great relationship with the animals, Adam, and God—but that wasn't enough for her. She believed the lie that there was something better out there . I do that myself sometimes when I scroll through Instagram. Everyone's highlight reel has a way of getting us to think that our lives aren't good enough—We should be vacationing more, have better clothes, have a different skin-care routine, a more fit bod, a nicer house, a cooler car, on and on. We often feel that God is holding out on us. But then if we bit into those apples, would that be enough?

King Solomon was a great example for this point of contentment. In the Song of Solomon, we see a young King

Solomon deeply in love with a Lebanese farm girl turned queen. In this book, Solomon gave poetic and sexual descriptions of a man and woman's anatomy and even described the physical intimacy they experienced in marriage. When we look at Ecclesiastes, we see that later, Solomon went on a journey to find meaning in life on his own; he looked into money, possessions, being kind, his work, and his accomplishments. He married seven hundred princesses and had three hundred concubines. Ecclesiastes 2:10–11 (NKJV) reads,

> Whatever my eyes desired I did not keep from them.
> I did not withhold my heart from any pleasure …
> indeed all was vanity and grasping for the wind.
> There was no profit under the sun.

The conclusion of his quest was this—Life means nothing if God's not in it. Ecclesiastes 12:1 (NKJV) tells us, "Remember now your Creator in the days of your youth. Before difficult days come." Ecclesiastes 12:13–14 (NKJV) reads, "Fear God and keep His commandments, for this is a man's all. For God will bring every work into judgment, Including every secret thing, weather good or evil." Solomon went from the simpleness of one love to having anyone and anything, but the more he filled himself with those lusts, the emptier he became.

Why are we the only creatures that wonder about life's meaning and purpose? Ecclesiastes 3:11 (NKJV) reads, "He has made everything beautiful in its time. Also He has put eternity in their hearts, except that no one can find out the work that God does from beginning to end." We crave to know because we were made to ask. God is good, and He has a plan. If we could figure out everything about God and His ways, we would be as sovereign as He is. He's the authority on life because He created it.

The late Ravi Zacharias verbally explained in the YouTube video "Why Did God Create the Tree of Good and Evil if He knew Adam and Eve Would Eat From it?" that the Creator had four options.

1. No world at all versus this world.
2. Creating a world where there would be no such thing as good and evil.
3. Creating a world where we would be predetermined to choose good.
4. Creating this world where there would be freedom to choose good or evil.

Ravi said that the fourth universe was the only option where love could exist. In option 1, we do not exist, so we cannot love. In option 2, love would be no different than hate. In option 3, we would exist as mindless love robots. In option 4, we are given the freedom to choose who and what we will love; in it is a relationship offered between Creator and creation and the ability to accept or reject His love.[1]

God was never trying to aggravate or exhaust fallen people by giving them free will; He was looking for genuine responses and is willing to run the risk of our rejecting Him to give us that.

CHAPTER 9

RUDE ATTITUDE

(Keeps No Record of Wrongs)

D o onto others as you would have them do onto you—The idea of the golden rule is in Matthew 7:12. It's a great idea, but do we live by it?

The year 2020 was supposed to be the year of vision, and for the first time, I saw how deeply divided America had become. We have begun to live in an "eye for an eye" society in which rudeness is accepted because the other person started it and we were just standing up for ourselves.

I was listening to the Lazy Genius podcast today; the topic was "Loving People You Disagree With." Kendra had a beautiful discussion about how to react when our passions didn't line up with our loved ones' passions: "Number one, remember what matters. What matters between you and this person you disagree with, is the love that you have for each other."

There is such thing as healthy discussion. Just because you disagree does not mean you cannot love and respect one another. There is such a thing as fighting fair, and in a healthy relationship, you should feel free to voice your opinions.

Number two was, "Choose narration over narratives." Kendra had heard this saying from Hillary McBride and shared how this idea became valid in her life. When you feel conflict arising,

> stop to notice your reaction and rather than letting that reaction fuel the narratives in your mind like "They just don't understand. I should've have just kept my mouth shut. How can they say they love me when they talk to me like this?" Rather than letting those thoughts run the show, choose narration instead.

Self-awareness is key when it comes to tactful disputes. Narration helps explain what is going on; inward narratives speak to how you are feeling.[1]

I'll give you an example of this to show how our natural responses can fail when our emotions want to override reason. I live in northern Minnesota, where deer hunting is a big deal. For most people, it's the Christmas that comes before Christmas. My kids even get a day off school, which has been deemed Deer Monday.

This deer season, I shot a monster buck—the one I had been waiting to shoot for thirteen years. I was pumped. My husband was pumped. My kids were pumped. We walked up to the deer, and Darby, my elated husband, wanted to take a picture of me with it. I thought about how I looked. I knew this picture would probably end up on Facebook and no doubt sent to his friends. As fear was washing over me, I said *"Umm ...* Can you take me back to the house first so I can put a little makeup on?"

He took me back to the house, and while I was in the bathroom, he called his dad. When his dad asked for a picture, Darby said he didn't have one because I had to put on some makeup first. I practically heard his dad's eyes rolling. My insecurities were popping up all over the place, and I responded in that way too. I asked Darby, "Why did you have to tell your dad that? Now he probably thinks I'm so vain!"

My husband then reacted in a likely manner. "You should be happy right now. You just got one of the biggest bucks I've ever seen, but no—Instead, you're mad about what I said to my dad!"

After that response, I did my normal thing ... I shut down and went into my inner narratives: *Did he tell his dad that multiple times in spite of the fact that I've been told I look like a boy if I'm not wearing makeup? I use makeup to look good for him too, not just me. He doesn't understand what it's like being a girl. He doesn't understand me. I'm not mad. I'm embarrassed. My feelings aren't valid to him. If he thinks I should be happy, then I have to be regardless of the circumstances?*

First of all, I failed to see the real issue and recognize why I was feeling as I did. My inner narratives took over my thoughts, and I projected them on others while exposing my insecurities. To take control of the situation, I began to justify my actions, and I came to the conclusion that I wasn't at fault. My conclusion was false, and the facts of our relationship prove that. Darby constantly tells me how beautiful I am in any and every state I've been in. He is really actually borderline obsessed with my physical features, and I'm not complaining. I failed to give Darby the insight he needed for my feelings, and yet I wanted him to understand. I should have told him how it made me feel and explained my reasoning.

Every relationship meets conflict, but healthy conflict does not try only to convince; it also tries to understand. We must learn to communicate with ourselves and others in healthy ways. When love is the objective, understanding can be the outcome. The Bible speaks about how we should behave and respond when conflict arises; being rude is out of the question.

First, Jesus tells us not to be hypocrites and to check ourselves and deal with our issues first before trying to help others with theirs. In Matthew 7:3–5 (NKJV), Jesus said,

> And why do you look at the speck in your brother's eye, but do not consider the plank in your own eye? Or how can you say to your brother "Let me remove the speck from your eye"; and then look, a plank is in your own eye? Hypocrite! First remove the plank from your own eye, and then you will see clearly to remove the speck from your brother's eye.

A few verses later, He laid out the golden rule. The sequence of this passage is important because when we learn to look within first, we discover the way we would like to be treated. That insight then helps us become the persons we wish we would have been in our moments of difficulty.

Second, we must learn to listen. Proverbs 18:13 (MSG) says, "Answering before listening is both stupid and rude." No one likes to be told how he or she should feel. Ask questions and listen for the answer. Don't act as if you know how someone should feel when you aren't in that person's position. James 1:19 (ESV) says, "Know this, my beloved brothers: let every person be quick to hear, slow to speak, slow to anger." Their feelings don't negate yours, so there is no reason to feel offended or get angry. If they don't understand even after you explain yourself, know that it's okay to drop the matter. Don't let someone else's emotions determine yours.

Last, our goal should be reconciliation. God is a God of relationships, and in Romans 12:9–21 (NKJV), Paul explained how we should conduct ourselves in them.

> Let love be without hypocrisy. Abhor what is evil. Cling to what is good. Be kindly affectionate to one another with brotherly love, in honor giving preference to one another; not lagging in diligence, fervent spirit, serving the Lord; rejoicing in hope, patient in tribulation, continuing steadfastly in prayer; distributing to the needs of the saints, given to hospitality. Bless those who persecute you; bless and do not curse. Rejoice with those who rejoice, and weep with those who weep. Be of the same mind toward one another. Do not set your mind on high things, but associate with the humble. Do not be wise in your own opinion. Repay no one evil for evil. Have regard for good things in the sight of all men. If it is possible live peaceably with all men. Beloved do not avenge yourselves, but rather give place to wrath; for it is written, "Vengeance is Mine, I will repay," says the Lord. Therefore "If your enemy is hungry, feed him; If he is thirsty, give him a drink; For in doing so you will heap coals of fire on his head." Do not be overcome by evil, but overcome evil with good.

So we are not to be hypocrites. We are to oppose evil and defend good. We are to be kind and unselfish and do things that bond us to others. We are to be sensitive to others and share in their emotions, but we are not to tell them how they should feel. We are to be humble and kind even with those who are unkind to us. Not everyone will have the same values we do, but we can try to live in peace. God sees everything, and He will right the wrongs. So if they persist in their hate, persist in your love. It's the only way to overcome evil.

Martin Luther King Jr. was perhaps one of the most influential voices on the subject of loving in truth. He stood his ground without stooping to the levels of his adversaries. The issues we face in the world today have become racially, religiously, and politically intertwined. It can be hard not to confuse acceptance with tolerance. God is just, and He shows us through Jesus Christ how it is possible to defend our positions by hating evil but not the evildoer. Love doesn't behave rudely because it knows that isn't how we get people to understand. Love stands on truth while stepping forward with grace, and it persists walking in that direction even when the winds of opposition are strong.

CHAPTER 10

THE DEVIL MADE ME DO IT

(Love Does Not Delight in Evil)

n the medical field,

> Contrast is important because it helps radiologists distinguish between normal and abnormal conditions. This helps them to see what is going on inside of you better. In turn, this allows them to make a more accurate diagnosis, and recommend the best treatment for your specific case.[1]

Those with acute myeloid leukemia typically undergo stem cell transplants. Doctors use chemo or radiation to kill the leukemia cells, but the high doses required also destroy bone marrow. Doctors then find someone who is a close match in terms of DNA so they can transplant some bone marrow. Being matched is miraculous in and of itself. Some patients have only one perfect match to count on, and some don't find matches at all.

If I were to get a transplant, my original DNA would say white, twenty-eight-year-old female, but my new blood stem cells would be reproducing my donor's DNA. Doctors and nurses refer to this process as having a new birth because they basically get patients close enough to death to destroy the cancer but then bring them back to life with new bone marrow.[2]

It is the perfect picture of salvation. There is a cancer running through humanity's veins called sin, and our perfect match is Jesus Christ. But if the cancer (sin) is not diagnosed properly, it will never be treated. This cancer does not cure itself, and it is internal. If you are willing to admit that no one is perfect, why is it so hard to call that imperfection sin? It's like calling someone with terminal cancer sick; sick may sound better than cancer, but it fails to explain its severity.

When we look internally, do we see perfection? No. Even nonbelievers are more than ready to admit that humans aren't perfect. The problem is that we hold ourselves up to other imperfect people to draw conclusions about what type of people we are. I'm not as bad as Hitler, but I haven't helped as many people as Mother Teresa; I'm just an average good person. It would be impossible for me to know for sure I was going to heaven based on a good and evil scale. I would constantly be unsure of my position in heaven, and that is why God puts our hearts on His scale, not our goodness. He holds us up to the perfectness of Jesus so we can see what we are lacking, not to make us feel hopeless.

It is not a sin to be tempted. Jesus was tempted by Satan, yet

He resisted. God gives us that same gift of choice. Matthew 4:1–11 (NKJV) tells us,

> Then Jesus was led up by the Spirit into the wilderness to be tempted by the devil. And when He had fasted forty days and forty nights, afterward He was hungry. Now when the tempter came to Him, he said, "If you are the Son of God, command that these stones become bread."
>
> But he answered and said, "It is written, Man shall not live on bread alone, but by every word that proceeds from the mouth of God."
>
> Then the devil took Him up into the holy city, set Him on the pinnacle of the temple and said to Him, "If you are the Son of God, throw yourself down. For it is written: 'He shall give His angels charge over you,' and, 'In their hands they shall bear you up, lest you dash your foot against a stone.'"
>
> Jesus said to him, "It is written again, you shall not tempt the Lord your God."
>
> Again, the devil took Him up on an exceedingly high mountain, and showed Him all the kingdoms of the world and their glory. And he said to Him, "All these things I will give You if You fall down and worship me."
>
> Then Jesus said to him, "Away with you, Satan! For it is written 'You shall worship the Lord your God and Him only shall you serve.'"
>
> Then the devil left Him and the angels came and ministered to Him.

A good enemy knows when to attack. This story says that Jesus was hungry. When we are hungry, we are vulnerable to feeding our desires with a quick fix instead of choosing lasting nourishment.

Let's give that a modern dialogue that speaks more to what we are lacking.

Adversary: Who are you? Are you lonely?

Us: Idk. I'm lonely.

Adversary: Well then, be what they want you to be. Here's a sexy dress and a drink to loosen you up. Let's go out and fill that void.

Next, he took Him to holy city and set Him up at the top telling Him to cast Himself off and that God would send angels to catch Him. Jesus knew that God would lift Him up but that He had to walk in God's will and avoid stumbling blocks set by Satan so God could use Him.

Adversary: Who are you? If you are Christian, you have nothing to fear. No matter what you do, God will love you because you are His child.

Us: Yeah, He will, but I want Him to be able to use me. God told me that if I do this, there would be consequences that would hurt me and those I love.

Finally, the devil took Him to the highest place and told Him he would give Him whatever He wanted as long as He worshipped him. Jesus told him to get away and that God would be the only one He would serve, and Satan left.

Adversary: God will make you wait, but I can give you whatever you want right now. All you have to do is listen to me and what I tell you. I can teach you if you'll let me.

Us: Away with you, Adversary!

Appealing isn't it? At times, I have been deceived into thinking Satan was right and could give me what he was promising, but his promises provide only momentary satisfaction. Jesus is the perfect contrast for human life because He is perfect and we aren't. If human blood has the power to cleanse and heal, imagine what His blood shed on the cross can do.

God promises us eternal satisfaction even though it may mean enduring discomforts in this vapor of a life. Ezekiel 36:23 (NIV) says, "I will give you a new heart and put a new spirit in you; I will remove from you your heart of stone and give you a heart of flesh." A stone is dead, but flesh is alive. God changes our hearts when we accept the gift of the Holy Spirit. Romans 10:9 (NIV) reads, "If you declare with your mouth, 'Jesus is Lord,' and believe in your heart that God raised Him from the dead, you will be saved." Saved from what? Death. Romans 6:23 (NIV) tells us, "For the wages of sin is death, but the gift of God is eternal life in Christ Jesus our Lord." Jesus is my donor, and His blood has the power to cleanse me. This new birth allows God to see Jesus when He looks at me. The gift from God to humanity is eternity, and Jesus willingly provided the way.

I WIN, YOU LOSE

(Rejoices with the Truth)

When it rains, it pours. That seemed to be what happened in my life five years ago. Months before I was due with my third child, my dad got very ill and was hospitalized. At first, they thought he had diverticulosis, but then they discovered it was a tumor.

A few months later, as the doctors prepared to go in and remove this golf ball–sized growth, they were very optimistic. They thought the mass was cancerous, but they didn't know the severity. They said surgery wouldn't take long and the recovery should go well.

But an hour turned into hours. The tumor they removed was the size of a softball, and they had to scrape off a spot on his liver. My father had stage-four colon cancer.

After his surgery, I had to drag myself to the hospital. I knew he was in bad shape, and I didn't want to see him like that. I couldn't eat. I couldn't sleep. I was shaking as I entered his room. I saw a man who looked nothing like my father. He was so weak and in so much pain that he could barely speak. But as tears filled his eyes, he uttered the words, "It's genetic." In his pain, he was thinking of what he had possibly passed on to my brother and me.

I looked away and choked back tears. I composed myself and looked at him. "It's okay, Dad. I love you." I gave my husband a signal that I wanted to leave. I don't think I lasted even five minutes in his room that night. I couldn't get back to the car fast enough. When my husband got in beside me, he grabbed my hand and said, "It's going to be okay, De."

"No it's not!" I said bursting into tears. "Did you see him? He looked terrible. He was in so much pain!"

We were quiet on the ride home. My usual glass half-full mentality was met with a negative reality that I didn't know how to overcome.

That night and following nights, I thought about why God would allow this. I prayed for my dad's life. God would grant me that wish, but I would have to go through many more months of watching him suffer, and that perhaps was the most painful part of all.

Anyone who has been through medical issues knows that they can put a huge strain on a family not just financially but also mentally. As the vortex of pain and unknown future started to swirl, things broke loose on the home front. It took only a few months of chemo before my dad wasn't up to his normal tasks on the family farm; his chores fell on my brother and mother. During the first few months, my mom was feeling very misunderstood as countless people tried to tell her what she should be doing and how she should feel. She was frustrated with the slowness of my dad's recovery and the responsibility of doing my dad's job as well as her own. She and my brother were headed into the busy season of calving, and I was about deliver a baby myself.

One morning at home, I had a gush of fluid and thought my water had broken. It was the beginning of March, and my due date wasn't until April 14, much too early for my water breaking. Because I wasn't having any contractions, I decided not to go in right that minute; I had a regular appointment the next day.

At that appointment, my doctor did blood work and an ultrasound just to make sure everything was good. The baby looked healthy, and I had a good amount of amniotic fluid, but his head was measuring two weeks bigger than his body, and that of course was a sign of Down syndrome. My heart sank as I thought about what that might mean for my life, but I was determined to love this baby no matter what.

A few days after the initial scare of my water breaking, it happened to me again and more than once that time. When I got to the hospital that night, I wasn't dilated. As the night went on, I kept on having gushes though they weren't testing positive for amniotic fluid. But I started dilating and was at four centimeters. Legally, they couldn't keep my baby at our rural hospital because they had no premature care available. I was at under thirty-eight weeks, and the staff was calling my status labor because of the dilation.

The doctor and nurse argued over whether to keep me there or fly me out. If I stayed, it would mean that my baby would be sent to a hospital two and a half hours away. My husband and I asked them to let us all go together, and finally, the nurse made a bold move and called in the Valley Med flight.

The flight staff was amazing; they were so calming and

professional, and they kept on feeding me encouraging little phrases. During the flight, my husband asked the pilot, "How much do these flights usually cost?"

"About forty to fifty thousand depending on your insurance," the pilot said.

I felt sick. That was just the fee for the flight, not the hospital stay or ambulance ride, and we hadn't met our deductible since it was a relatively new year. We had been saving up for a new house for five years, and numbers like that would wipe out our nest egg and more. I prayed for the rest of the flight for our baby, my dad, and our finances.

When I arrived at the new hospital, nurses and doctors were puzzled by my rare performance; I persistently told them that I wasn't wetting myself. A couple of nurses at the last hospital even smelled one of my pads to try figure out what the fluid was, and even they agreed it wasn't urine. They checked my cervix, and I was dilated one centimeter more. I kept having gushes. The fluid had blood mixed with it, but it still tested negative for amniotic fluid.

The next morning, the doctor told me, "I still don't know where this fluid is coming from, but one of your tests this morning came back positive. You've been at this long enough. We'll break your water and start you on Pitocin if needed."

As she went to break my water, she looked up and said, "*Hmmm* … That's strange. It's practically empty. There's hardly any fluid in it."

I remembered what it was like with my first child when they broke my water—splash pad city, not the trickle I had just experienced. I was lucky that infection hadn't set in; they typically say you're supposed to deliver twenty-four hours after your water breaks to prevent that.

I'll spare you the delivery details and skip to the part where he was laid on my chest and I gazed at his perfection. Ten fingers, ten toes, cute little button nose, and the whitest blond hair. After watching him for a bit, I realized that his breathing rate was unusually rapid. They abruptly took him away and listened to his lungs. Something wasn't right. The doctor explained that his lungs were underdeveloped and that he would need a feeding tube and oxygen for the time being.

As they hauled him off to the NICU, I was moved to another room. I was in a lot of pain physically and emotionally. They told me I needed to rest; I couldn't see my baby until the morning. I couldn't sleep. There was also another thing heavy on my heart and mind; the day that I had Thor was the same day my dad had his first chemo treatment.

When I was wheeled into the NICU the next morning, I knew which one my baby was right away. He looked like a giant! All these less than five-pound babies surrounded my seven-pounder. I was so grateful to see him, and it was hard not to hold him.

Days went by, and he still needed assistance, so we had to move to a hotel. Darby and I cried the first night in our room thinking about how much we missed our two girls at home. It had been a week since we had seen them, and because of influenza restrictions at the hospital, they couldn't meet their brother. Darby needed to go back to work; I told him I couldn't leave my baby.

Night after night, I went back to the hotel alone and set my alarm for all the visits. I could hold him only every three hours for less than fifteen minutes because he at that point needed to be under a light to treat his jaundice. After fourteen long days in the NICU, he came home with me!

When I first returned to my parents' house, my girls were

enthralled with their baby brother. I went over to the kitchen table to sit with my dad. He slid a newspaper in my direction and pointed to an article telling me to read it. The article explained that because of our remote location, starting on March 1, Valley Med flights would be free in our county. I'd been flown out March 8, and Thor had been born on March 9, but the first time I went in with my water leaking, it was still February. God had me. God had this. A wave of peace rushed over me. If God could hold me through all that, He could hold me through my dad's cancer journey even if the five-year survival rate for his condition was only 16 percent. I had hope he would defy the odds.

Throughout the next months, our family bonded in a way we hadn't before, and my dad was changing too. Because of our hard journey, we had seen the hand of God and realized the peace that passed all understanding.

My dad has been cancer free for five years now, and he takes vacations much more now than he ever did. We all see life, family, friends, and community in a different light. Suffering grew us in a way that nothing else could have.

Jeremiah 17:5–8 (ESV) reads,

> Thus says the Lord: "Cursed is the man who trusts in man and makes flesh his strength, whose heart departs from the Lord. For he shall be like a shrub in the desert, and shall not see when good comes, but shall inhabit the parched places in the wilderness, in a salt land which is not inhabited. Blessed is the man who trusts in the Lord, and who's hope is in the Lord. For he shall be like a tree planted by the waters, which spreads out its roots by the river,

and will not fear when heat comes; but its leaf will be green, and will not be anxious in the year of drought, nor will it cease to yield fruit."

The first part of this verse could be rephrased into modern terms like this. If you are trusting yourself and your strength in this life, don't be surprised if you cannot see the good things when they come along. Without God, hope is a mirage. You will constantly be lost and tired when you're chasing an optical illusion.

The pain of those turbulent moments was very real, but the peace that rushed over me every time I gave it to God in prayer was unexplainable. I realized that my faith wasn't rooted in my dad or my son and that if life decided to take those things away, everything would still be okay. I knew that even if I did have to endure the pain of those losses, I would one day get to see them in heaven.

Death does not have the power to part the love we can feel for someone; that's why loss hurts so much. God's love for us is the same. It's eternal, but we can separate ourselves from His love, and that separation hurts. Jesus is the compass for the destination of God's love. In 1 John 4:18 (NKJV), we read, "There is no fear in love, but perfect love casts our fear, because fear involves torment, but he who fears has not been made perfect in love."

God isn't a tyrannical ruler. He isn't out to get you, and He doesn't rejoice in your iniquity. He grieves with you and cares about you. Love wouldn't have it any other way. If you are going through hard times, don't fear them; give the situation to Him and trust Him to turn it into good. Your painful path has the potential to be more rewarding than you could've ever imagined. If you lean on God during turbulent times, He will comfort and love you throughout the storm.

CHAPTER 12

THE TRUTH

(Love Always Protects)

I t was a cherished weekend away in the city to celebrate my childhood friend Katie's first baby. The night before her baby shower, we met up with friends and enjoyed good food, drinks, and company. As the night came to a close, I followed GPS navigation to my sister-in-law's house, where I would be staying. Because it was late and they were going to bed, she said that she'd just keep their apartment's sliding door unlocked so I could just come in.

I arrived, grabbed my little rollie suitcase, walked up to the apartment, and tugged on the sliding door. It slid open, and I poked my head into the plastic blinds, which banged against each other like wind chimes. I pulled myself and my luggage the rest of the way through. The light from the street lit up the room enough for me to notice that they had rearranged things and had gotten some new furniture. As I went to open the door to the room I would be staying in, I heard the dog locked in the pantry whining. That was strange because they usually left her free to roam around the place. I shrugged off the weird but little changes and continued on my journey. As I entered the bedroom, I didn't turn on a light because the shades were open and were letting enough light through.

I then noticed that this room had also been rearranged and had new furniture. The bed was bigger, and it had a lump in it. I decided that it was most likely their son, Lincoln. I plopped my bag down and began to crawl up on the end of the bed repeating his name over and over: "Lincoln? Lincoln?"

A startled man-child emerged from the sheets and connected himself to the wall like a cat crawling up curtains. His eyes had sheer terror in them, and his mouth was agape but silent. I jumped back, grabbed my bag, and walked backward toward the door apologizing profusely in the calmest manner possible. "Oh my goodness! I'm so sorry! I'm in the wrong house. Please excuse me!"

I shut the door as gingerly as possible and turned to run out. My bag flopped from side to side and eventually off its wheels. Dragging it behind me, I crashed my way to the door, pulled it open, and catapulted myself through it. I ran back to my car still dragging my bag laughing hysterically as I pictured that young man telling his roommate the next morning about some girl who had walked into his room and the two of them trying to figure out if it was real or a dream and then looking out the window and seeing the path through the snow I had made. I called my sister-in-law to ask her once again where her apartment was, and half-asleep, she informed me that I had turned one street too early.

I realized I could have avoided the whole situation if I had turned on the lights; I would have clearly seen that I was in the wrong house.

In Genesis 1:3–4 (NKJV), God said, "'Let there be light'; and there was light. And God saw the light and that it was good; and God divided the light from the darkness." Scientists adhere to the fact that this is what happened at the beginning of time; they just don't credit God as the one who did it.

In the first three verses of the Bible, we see God the Father creating the heavens and earth, God the Spirit hovering over the face of the waters, and God the Son (the Word) speaking light and dividing the light from the darkness. These three entities all did one thing; they showed the glory of God. As the Father created, the Spirit reflected and the Son spoke. Life began in and through them.

John 1:1–5 (NKJV) says,

> In the beginning was the Word and the Word was with God, and the Word was God. He was in the beginning with God. All things were made through Him and without Him nothing was made that was made. In Him was life, and the life was the light of men. And the light shines in the darkness, and the darkness did not comprehend it.

God showed Paul that His reference in Genesis to creation had spiritual significance for humankind as well: "For God, who said 'Let light shine out of darkness,' has shone in our hearts to give the light of the knowledge of the glory of God in the face of Jesus Christ" (2 Corinthians 4:6 ESV). Before God said, "Let there be light," He had already shaped the heavens and earth. Then He began to give the earth order and purpose. Paul said that enlightenment had been given to humanity through Jesus Christ. God had separated the darkness from the light cosmically through the Word, and He does the same spiritually through Jesus. Jesus is referred to in the Bible as the light of the world, and the term *Christian* means Christlike.

The Christian hope hangs on the facts that Jesus was God in human form and that He lived, died, and rose again. Paul said in 1 Corinthians 15:14 (NIV), "If Christ has not been raised, our preaching is useless and so is your faith." Jesus said He would prove He was the Son of God by raising Himself from the dead. If He didn't do that, He was a liar and a fake.

John 1:14 (NKJV) reads, "And the Word became flesh and dwelt among us, and we beheld His glory, the glory as of the only begotten of the Father, full of grace and truth." God became tangible through His Son, Jesus. John, who wrote this verse, was one of Jesus's best friends. He didn't only see Him; he got to walk through life with Him.

In 1 John 1:1–2 (NKJV), John said,

> That which was from the beginning, which we have heard, which we have seen with our eyes, which we have looked upon, which our hands have handled concerning the Word of life … we have seen and bear witness, and declare to you.

John was saying, "Look … We've seen Jesus. We looked at Him, touched Him, and have heard Him. They saw Him crucified and then alive again. He isn't just a fantasy or a philosophy; He's real." John believed He was who He said He was, and the disciples were there to tell them about the encounters they had with Jesus even when their declarations of their faith in Jesus put them in great danger. Most of the disciples were killed and imprisoned for speaking of their faith in Jesus Christ as the one true God. People die for their faith only if it is something they truly believe in.

We have already looked into the fact that Jesus lived, but did He really die? Perhaps the most telling detail of Jesus's death is recorded in John 19:34 (NKJV): "One of the soldiers pierced Jesus' side with a spear, bringing a sudden flow of blood and water." This medical phenomenon of blood separating happens after death occurs.[1] Jesus would have had to have been dead for a while before they pierced His side for this to occur. Since red blood cells are heavier than plasma, they would have sunk to the bottom of Jesus's thorax. When the spear was withdrawn from His thorax, blood would have come out first before plasma, a lighter substance, did.

Think of it like water and oil in a jar that mix when we shake it but that separate when we let it sit. If we punctured a hole in the jar, first, water would come out and then the oil. It would have been impossible for this to be faked, and the medical significance was unknown during that era, so writers wouldn't have even thought to put this in as proof that Jesus actually died.

This was not only a recorded bodily function but also a significant spiritual picture. The Bible says that when we put our faith in Christ, "the blood of Jesus, His Son, purifies us from all sin" (1 John 1:7 NIV). Romans 6:4 (NKJV) says, "We were therefore buried with Him through baptism into death, that just as Christ was raised from the dead by the glory of the Father, even so we should walk in the newness of life." The symbols of blood and water give us a picture of how Jesus gave us new life through His death, burial, and resurrection. Romans 10:9 (NIV) says, "If you declare with your mouth 'Jesus is Lord,' and Believe in your heart that God raised Him from the dead, you will be saved."

Jesus appeared to over five hundred people in His resurrected body weeks after His death, and the first people He appeared to were women. Believing a woman's testimony in that era would've been social suicide, but it wasn't only believed; it was written. The writers of the Bible wrote the events as they happened regardless of how they were perceived by society. They were committed to telling the truth even when it meant exposing their failures as God's people.[2]

The skeptic Thomas stood in a room multiple times with the resurrected Jesus. Even though everyone else believed Jesus was who He said He was, Thomas wasn't sure. Jesus knew Thomas didn't fully believe that He was the same Jesus who had died on the cross. Jesus spoke with Thomas in John 20:27–29 (NKJV).

> "Reach your finger here, and look at My hands; reach your hand here, and put it into my side. Do not be unbelieving, but believing." And Thomas answered and said to Him, "My Lord and my God!" Jesus said to Him, "Thomas, because you have seen Me, you have believed. Blessed are those who have not seen and yet have believed."

If you are doubting, don't be afraid to pray and ask God to reveal Himself to you. If you genuinely want to know who He is, He will show you. He isn't going to reprimand you for asking; He wants you to be enlightened. To learn the truth, you have to be brave enough to ask the questions and humble enough to receive the answers He gives regardless of your preconceived ideologies.

Some faiths put the sole responsibility on you and what you accomplish in life, but the Christian faith puts it on Christ and the work He did on the cross. Yes, we are called to show the work of Christ in us and share what God has done for us, but God doesn't ask for performance or perfection but authenticity.

The Bible is filled with men and women of God who failed to uphold Christlike standards. Jacob was a deceiver … Moses killed an Egyptian … David slept with a married woman and then killed her husband … Paul was first a persecutor and killed Christians … Sarah beat her servant for her own mistake … This list could go on and on. One thing God's people in the Bible had in common was how they failed forward; they didn't stay in their guilt and shame, and even though there were consequences, when they returned to God and did things His way, their lives were healed.

God knows we will fall and fail, but He asks us to get up and continue. He doesn't care if society has written us off; He doesn't want us living for people's approval anyway, and He isn't going to buy the excuse that we don't believe in God because of how some supposed Christians acted toward us. He can sympathize with that; after all, He was betrayed by one of His own, but if we look to others to show us who God is and they fail, which they will, God says that shows His grace, mercy, and forgiveness. It shows our inadequacies, not His.

John 3:16–21 (NKJV) says,

> For God so loved the World that He gave His only begotten Son that whosoever believes in Him should not perish but have everlasting life. For God did not send His Son into the world to condemn the world, but that the world through Him maybe saved. He who believes in Him is not condemned; but he who does not believe is condemned already, because he

has not believe in the name of the only begotten Son of God. And this is the condemnation, that the light has come into the world, and men loved darkness rather than light, because their deeds were evil. For everyone practicing evil hates the light and does not come to the light, lest his deeds should be exposed. But he who does the truth comes into the light, that his deeds maybe clearly seen, that they have been done in God.

When it comes to truth and being in the dark, sometimes, we see what we want to see, not what is actually there. In my previous story, all the signs that I was in the wrong house were right in front of me: the couches were rearranged, the dog was locked in the pantry instead of freely roaming around, there was a big bed in the bedroom instead of a small one. If I would've flipped on the lights, I would've seen clearly right away that this wasn't my sister-in-law's house, but I ignored my intuition the whole time.

Jesus was at the beginning of time being the light and life to humanity, but we couldn't see Him. Maybe you would not consider Jesus as a part of your life, but He has been present the whole time. He wants you to see Him, and he has revealed Himself to you through creation and the bible, but He's waiting for you to come into the light and examine the evidences.

Is this you today? If it is, pray and ask Him to reveal Himself to you. When He does, don't shy away from the truth He brings; go to His Word and seek Him. When He turns on the light, don't reside in the dark places you were never meant to be. Start searching for the place He is trying to lead you to—heaven. God gave us a Savior—Jesus Christ—for our protection.

CHAPTER 13

THE WHOLE TRUTH

(Love Always Trusts)

Truth is exclusive in its nature and can feel off-putting, but how we feel about truth has no effect on it. We must seek truth regardless of our ill feelings toward it. Whether we are trying to take God out of the universe or explain His existence in it, there are still unanswered questions that require elements of faith on both sides. I've learned to examine the evidence I can see instead of dwelling on the things I cannot conclude. Hebrews 11:1(NKJV) says, "Now faith is the substance of things hoped for, the evidence of things not seen."

Let's start with the truth in Genesis 1:1–2 (NKJV): "In the beginning God created the heavens and the earth. The earth was without form, and void." For years, astronomers thought that the world had always existed and did not have a beginning. In 1929, astronomer Edwin Hubble began to measure the relative distance between galaxies using light, and he noticed there were red shifts in the light; galaxies outside ours were moving away from us, and those that were the farthest away were moving the fastest. If we could reverse that mathematically, we would see all stars and galaxies collapsing back to the point of nothing. This gave evidence to the truth that the universe did have a beginning before which there was nothing.[1] Genesis was written by Moses in 1445 BC, 3,374 years before humans discovered that the universe had a beginning.

"For every material effect that we see, there has to be a cause that came before it or was greater than it."[2] An atheistic view claims that a single piece of matter came and produced the big bang, but where did that piece of matter originate? Famous theoretical physicist Stephen Hawking said, "Nothing caused the big bang ... Singularity arose from nothing."[3] In his book *The Grand Design*, Hawking claimed, "Bodies such as stars and black holes, can't appear out of nothing but a whole universe can."[4]

Bear with me in this next section as I dive deeper into the waters of quantum physics and try to swim. In *Brief Answers to Big Questions*, Hawking explained the possibility of a universe without a creator, but what is the probability of that? Roger Penrose of Oxford University said that the odds of this universe having happened by chance was 1 in 10 to the 10 to the 123. In case you are not sure what that means, the odds are astronomically low.[5] John C. Polkinghornea Quantum physicist, wrote in *One World*,

> When you look at the early days of the formation of
> the universe the expansion and contraction rate had
> to be so precise, and the margin of error so small,
> that it would be like taking aim at a 1 square inch

object at the other end of the universe 20 billion light years away and hitting it bullseye.[6]

And those are just the chances of our universe existing, not all life forms.

Isaiah 40:22 (NIV) says, "He sits enthroned above the circle of the earth." This was over 2,200 years before Magellan sailed around the world and proved that the earth was a sphere.

Job 26:7 (KJV) reads, "He stretcheth out the north over the empty place; and hangeth the earth upon nothing." The only thing that holds our earth in place is gravity; it hangs on nothing. In 2004, scientists discovered a super void in the southern hemisphere and just to the north an abode of stars.[7]

Science can find explanations for portions of life, but there are many factors that play into our complex existence. The Bible is scientifically, philosophically, historically, and geopolitically correct.

Let's look at the historical proofs of Jesus. Approximately 2,000 years ago, a man named Jesus was put to death on a hill called Mount Calvary because He claimed to be the Son of God. The Old Testament predicted His birth, death, and resurrection years before they occurred.

Jewish and Roman historians mentioned Jesus in their writings and accused Him of leading people astray calling Him a magician. They never denied His existence; their writings in fact lay claim to it. No matter their beliefs, the most accomplished historians say that Jesus of Nazareth was a real person in history. Historian Dr. Gary Habermas explained these truths and defended the Christian faith, but because he is a Christian, I will use a different source so religious bias cannot be claimed. Atheist and New Testament scholar Bart Ehrman gives historical evidence in his book *Did Jesus Exist?* and stated that all experts in the area agreed that "whatever else you may think about Jesus, he certainly did exist."[8]

People claim that testimonies are not important because they are just individuals' experiences, and I do believe that testimonies can be misleading and should not be the only reason to believe. Yet in the judicial realm, we use eyewitness accounts to corroborate findings.

J. Warner Wallace, an American homicide detective, explained in a seminar that when people were no longer living and there was little or no forensic evidence, other methods can be applied to discover truth. Wallace was an atheist for thirty-five years, and when he looked into God's crime scene, he found reasons to believe that the Christian faith was an anchor that gives hope to the soul for good reason. In the Gospels, he discovered something that was critical in any investigation—eyewitness accounts. Multiple witnesses who have seen the same event can testify to what they saw, but they might not tell the exact same story. In fact, if their stories are too similar, that could indicate that they may have been rehearsed. This is true in the Bible when you look at the variances between Matthew's, Mark's, and Luke's accounts. Detectives look at whether these different accounts have details that can be put together like a puzzle.

Wallace told a story about a woman known for drug addiction and bank robbing being found dead one morning in her bed. Crime scene pictures captured heroin needles and crack pipes littering her bedside table, and the police concluded that she had died of an overdose. But when the coroner got there and pulled back the sheets, he saw that she had been stabbed to death. The officers' presumptions had led them to false conclusions; they failed to dig deeper because they thought they already knew the answers.[9]

Beyond reasonable doubt is the standard we look at when judging a case. How do we determine what is reasonable? We look at the possibilities and began to cross off those that do not match up with the evidence.

In John 8:21–36 (NKJV), Jesus told others that He would be killed but would rise again and that that was how they would know He was the Son of God. John 8:31–32 (NKJV) says, "If you abide in My word, you are My disciples indeed. You shall know the truth and the truth shall make you free."

Perhaps you have misjudged Jesus based on others' opinions of Him, or perhaps your experiences with other Christians have caused your disbelief. Although Christians are supposed to be Christlike, we sometimes find the opposite of that. Even though I can sympathize with those feelings, I can't agree with the premise of the argument. Jesus never claimed that His people were perfect, and His character should be judged based on what He did.

To know Him and His words, you have to put in some time and effort. I like the scientific method steps—observe, question, research, hypothesize, experiment, test hypothesis, draw conclusion, report. Jeremiah 29:13 (NIV) reads, "You will seek me and find me when you seek me with all your heart." Do your own digging, and ask God to reveal Himself to you. If you do, you will uncover some answers to questions that you've buried. If that process becomes uncomfortable or painful, don't give up. Push through it and stay committed to developing a relationship and finding truth.

God has given me enough evidence to believe He exists. Trusting in Jesus and giving God my life have been the best decisions I've ever made, and trust is the emotional oxygen every relationship needs to live.

CHAPTER 14

NOTHING BUT THE TRUTH

(Love Always Hopes)

The new-age belief theory is a movement in religion that has captivated celebrities such as Oprah Winfrey and Tony Robbins. This ideology claims spirituality with no need for a god. New age says that you are god and have the power to manipulate the metaphysical world by using the law of attraction. It holds that the law of attraction uses the power of the mind to manifest your desired results. It says that when we align our inner world positively, the universe reacts positively. Like attracts like, so if we want a new outer world, we can create it.

New agers believe that the universe is good and gives only good things. Therefore, if we are aligned with the universe, we will get what we want. This also means that any negativity is out. Don't let any unsettling thoughts in, because if you do, your fears will become reality.[1]

Every belief system has some sort of beginning including founders and texts you can draw information from. The new age movement (NAM) although Western draws mostly from Eastern mysticism and early movements such as new thought, spiritualism, theosophy, and the occult.

A big contention between NAM and Christianity is their ideas on God. NAM rejects the idea of a loving, personal, knowable God. Instead of a theistic belief that God created everything, NAM holds a more pantheistic view that there are many gods and that we create our own realities. NAM differs from Eastern religions such as Hinduism and Buddhism, whose adherents believe in abstaining from many things to find nirvana or inherit rewards. NAM focuses on individuals as the center; they feed and fill their desires until their individual pictures of nirvana exist.

NAM uses sources such as meditation, crystals, yoga, diet, channeling, and cosmos and spirit guides to align its adherents with the universe and awaken god in human beings. It does not believe in evil; all sources are good and produce good, and "all paths lead to god."[2]

These are just a few of the questions I had when it came to this topic. Are this law and prayer basically the same thing? Christians pray to God to try to get what they want, don't they? What similarities do these belief systems have, or what divides them? Do I have the power to will anything I want into existence, or is this world controlled by someone other than me?

I'm going to expound and draw on the thoughts of Steven Bancarz, a former believer in the law of attraction, in the next section. In his YouTube video "The Law of Attraction Debunked," he broke down why he no longer thinks the law of attraction is good and gave possible reasons for why it sometimes works. He said,

If a person uses these Law of Attraction principles only one person will attain their desired result. On average a major lottery has around 1 million people participating. Out of those 1 million people say 1,000 people practice the theory and truly believe that they will win. Out of that 1% still only 1 person wins. In order for something to be a law, whenever those "right conditions" present themselves the reaction has to occur 100% of the time.[3]

Compare that outcome to the laws of chemistry; whenever we mix baking soda and vinegar, the same chemical reaction occurs. Positive thinking does not guarantee positive results.

I believe every good lie is based on a half-truth. When watching new agers' testimonies, I see that some of them are telling the truth about their positive experiences. I question though what source is giving them these incredible things. I noticed that most of the new-age testimonies talk about how the person has received things such as fame, power, and financial gain. And this is one of the major differences I found when comparing it to Christianity.

If you look at the "I Am Second" testimonies put up by White Chair Films, you notice a completely different kind of prosperity woven into these Christians' stories.[4] New agers claim to be spiritual, but their spiritual interaction produces more-materialistic results. Remember in chapter 10 when we looked at Jesus being tempted by Satan? Satan never offered Jesus internal prosperities such as love, joy, peace, or patience in return for His allegiance; he offered Him shortcuts to attaining kingdoms, power, and position.

Matthew 7:11 (NKJV) says, "If you then being evil, know how to give good gifts to your children, how much more will your

Father who is in heaven give good things to those who ask Him." God is more interested in giving us spiritual rather than material gifts, which can be taken away. What we put our faith in matters. If we align ourselves with the world's views, we will hold up what it considers important, but if we align ourselves with God, we will desire different things. Romans 12:2 (NLT) tells us,

> Don't copy the behavior and customs of this world, but let God transform you into a new person by changing the way you think. Then you will learn to know God's will for you, which is good and pleasing and perfect.

Let me introduce you to Nick Vujicic. This Australian has captured my heart, and though our stories look different, we draw water from the same stream. Nick was born without arms and legs. He talked about the emotion that went along with a disability like that. For the first four months after his birth, his parents went through grief and confusion no doubt wondering how a loving God could have allowed that. He was told he would never walk, never go to school. At age ten, he attempted suicide. His parents told him that they loved him, that he had a purpose, that he was special, but he told them that he didn't want to be special.

But Nick read the story of the blind man in John 9:1–12 (NIV), which talks about Jesus's encounter with a man who had been blind since birth. The disciples asked Jesus, "Rabbi, who sinned, this man or his parents, that he was born blind?" "Neither this man nor his parents sinned," said Jesus, "but this happened so that the works of God might be displayed in him." When Nick read that, he decided to give his life to Jesus so that he might be used by God as well.

Today, Nick can swim, golf, play soccer, drive, type faster than I can, and numerous other things. He says that our only disabilities are those of our hearts, that if you put the word *go* in front of the word *disable*, it spells "God is able."

He started Life without Limbs, a ministry, and he has shared the gospel all around the world with millions. He has a beautiful wife, four children, and a radiant joy. He has said that he knows that God can heal him. He has seen miracles happen and has experienced some himself. When asked if he had prayed for limbs, he said, "Yes, many times!" and he has a pair of shoes in his closet just in case God decides to do that. But he follows that up with, "If someone were to offer me a magic pill, though, that could give me that right now, I wouldn't take it." Nick wants blessings only from God, and he has seen and experienced the joy in unanswered prayers.[5]

Do you know the way that new age belief explains Nick's condition? He did something bad in a past life. A woman even told him that once in an airport. God explained it like this, though: "I made Nick like that so that I could show others my power. He is a blessed and beautiful work of art, and I love him." Nick is one of God's living, breathing miracles and an extension of His heart.

God never rejects your feelings, and Nick doesn't leave out the part of the story where he and his parents struggled, but they took their cares, fears, anxieties, and concerns to the right source of life. God doesn't tell us to put them out of our minds and act as if they aren't there; He said, "Therefore humble yourselves under the mighty hand of God, that He may exalt you in due time, casting all your cares upon Him for He cares for you" (1 Peter 5:6–7 NKJV).

God wants to hear from us especially when it's dark and we're unsure of our journey. He doesn't tell us that our difficult circumstances are hopeless; He assures us that they are the perfect place for Him to begin His work. He doesn't reprimand honest conversations from broken hearts; He invites them.

Nick said that it was not positive thinking that leads him but Jesus Christ and His redeeming work on the cross. What motivates Nick is the hope of value, purpose, identity, and destiny that only God can give.

Faith requires trust. God's hand may be unseen, but His mighty works are prevalent in our world today. If you do not trust that someone has your best interests in mind, you won't give him or her your heart. If you want to see God's faithfulness, you have to be willing to look at the lives He has touched. You need to listen to how He has changed them even if you cannot fully comprehend it. Then maybe one day, you'll experience it yourself.

CHAPTER 15

SO HELP ME GOD

(Love Always Perseveres)

I work in an industry that allows me to talk to people of different beliefs and life paths. One thing I have noticed is regret in the voices of people who were on good paths that turned into hard paths that caused them to prematurely give up. Florence Chadwick, a long-distance swimmer, once lived that story out.

In 1952, Florence Chadwick stepped into the chilling Pacific Ocean waters with great hopes of being the first woman to swim from Catalina Island to California's mainland. The morning was chilly, the wind was strong, and the fog was so thick that she could barely see the boats that were accompanying her.

Fifteen hours into her swim, she stopped; she was exhausted and cold. She cried out that she wanted to be done. Her mother, who was in one of the boats, called to her telling her to stick it out, she was almost there. Her mother could not see the shoreline but believed it was close.

The wind beating against Chadwick made her feel she was making little if any progress. She swam for another hour but then gave up. Moments later, as they drove through the fog at a more rapid pace, Florence saw the shoreline. She had gone twenty-five miles and had had only one mile to go.[1]

Sometimes, our misty eyes create a thick fog and we cannot see the shoreline. We feel physically, emotionally, and spiritually drained. As the winds beat against our faces and push us from opposing directions, we begin to break. Imagine though if we were able to keep on swimming despite our momentary inability to see clearly. In 1 Corinthians 13:12 (NKJV), we read, "For now we see in a mirror, dimly, but then face to face. Now I know in part, but then I shall know just as I also am known." I don't have all the answers now, but I believe one day I will.

I know who I would be without the work of the Lord in my life. It's not a pretty picture. I'm a selfish, devious, impatient, wild child who would have been swallowed up in my own wake. I most likely would have never married my husband, and if I had, I'd probably be divorced by now. I was the life of the party with a desire to please, but I always left feeling used, broken, and lonely. Bad guys were my thing; they were exciting and not afraid of me, but they also never really cared about my needs. I fell in love with Darby, the opposite of that. He is a total teddy bear who played on the safe side almost all his life. *Rebel* was not a term anyone would ever use for him.

I say "bad guys" carefully. Everyone is flawed and therefore has good as well as bad character traits. My friend recently used a line that I love: "It's all about feeding the right dog." Darby spent his teen and young adult life pretty much doing that—making selfless choices and not using women for his pleasure. He would not walk into friendships asking what others could do for him but what he could do for them. Good decisions lead to good life choices, which lead to the character trait of integrity.

We've been married for ten years now, but I almost ended it after our second date when he told me that he loved me. I know, it's weird to criticize this, but as I was driving home that night, all I could think was, *He doesn't love me. He doesn't even know me!*

I didn't realize it then, but I put him to the test for a year. Every time he said, "I love you," I'd just give him a smile or a nod or even a thanks (lol—so cringy). I remember him asking me once, "Why don't you ever say it back? Don't you love me?"

"Yeah, I think I do," I said, "but I never want to say that to someone unless I'm sure I won't ever stop loving him. I never want to have to take it back." That's what I said, but what I really meant was, *If you ever break up with me, I don't want you to have the power of saying you broke my heart.* Love was a game I wasn't going to lose at. I didn't tell him I loved him because I didn't believe he truly loved me yet. At least not until I tested that love and he chose to stay.

The look on his face after that statement was an *I should probably break up with her,* but he didn't. Darby kept on loving me, and eventually, I did say it back.

However, at age twenty-six and after seven years of marriage, I became insecure and very unsure of my identity, and I was about to put Darby's love to the test again. I thought about all the things people had told me and came to the conclusion that I wasn't enough. I compared myself to others and decided I needed to change myself. Some things I used to be able to push past such as others' opinions started unsettling me. I went to all my insecure places and asked myself if what other people had labeled me was true. I felt like that girl in gym class who was always picked last. Weak, ugly, dumb, and weird—that was what I began to think I was because those were titles others had tagged me with at some point or other.

I was falling short of every expectation I had set for myself as a wife, mother, daughter, friend, and Christian. Every failure rang through my head until I believed the lies that I didn't deserve to be loved and that I wasn't ever going to be good enough to carry those titles.

One night during that time, Darby rolled over in bed and said, "De, you're seriously so perfect. I love you so much."

The words almost angered me. *Why does he say that when he knows I'm not?* I thought. *I mean, it's marriage. He's seen my every flaw over and over. Why does he think I'm perfect?* With tears rolling down my cheeks, I asked him, "How could you love someone like me?"

"What do you mean?" he asked.

"I mean, you act like I'm the best thing that ever happened to you, the most beautiful thing you've ever seen, but I'm not. I'm not perfect!"

He looked at me confused. He brushed my tears away and said, "I wish you could see yourself through my eyes."

I realized then that it wasn't other people who didn't love me but me who didn't believe I was worthy of love, so I had never really accepted it. I looked into Darby's eyes and saw the truth that he loved me in spite of my flaws and he wasn't going anywhere. Love had never left me; I had left love. Darby saw my flaws and failures but looked at me through the lens of love. He was not my parents, who I felt were obligated to love me. He was not a friend who could take me or leave me. He was not staying with me because he had to. He did not pick me because he had no other options. He wanted to be with me.

I realized that if Darby could love me like that, a perfect and holy God could too. Loving in spite of flaws was what I had been taught about God's love for His creation, and I was experiencing it through my husband's love for me. It does not mean God condones hurtful behavior, but He guides us to love with integrity, mercy, and grace. A good relationship with Darby didn't require my perfection, but there are things I could do to break the relationship. Love doesn't naturally flourish; it will always take effort and dedication from both parties.

Psalm 73:26 (NIV) reads, "My flesh and my heart will fail, but God is the strength of my heart and my portion forever."

At that point, I felt strongly that God had given me enough evidence to conclude that He wasn't a fable and that Jesus Christ was His Son. I was thankful for those answers, but I still questioned God about why He had allowed some of the hurt in my life to continue. I had prayed that God would use me in a mighty way, but I didn't feel He was. I asked Him to deliver me from the deep depression I was in, but He didn't. I prayed for a big job and a purpose, a distraction from my pain, but He wouldn't give me that.

I didn't want to fold laundry every day and pick up the house as my kids destroyed it. I didn't want to live this mundane mom life day after day. I wanted adventure and excitement. I wanted what I had defined as happiness.

That led me to my next journey. I decided that if God wouldn't give me my fantasy life, I'd go get it myself, but when people didn't follow suit and crushed my fantasy, I got angry. I packed my schedule as full as I could. God allowed me to do all the things I thought would make me happy. I was adventuring and having fun; I was getting hired for art jobs. I dove into anything that looked or sounded like the golden ticket out of depression. At times, I felt waves of relief and joy, but the deep sadness would again flood my emotions just minutes later. I couldn't keep the joy coming.

One weekend as I sat on the grass of a beautiful summer home watching my kids play and soaking up the sun, I prayed, "God, why isn't this enough?" A recurring phrase passed through my mind: "Because, De, your fantasy life is built on human pleasures, and those fade away. My purpose for you is built on foundations that are eternal. Stop trying to jump ahead of me. Just wait. In my timing, I'll give you what you ask."

I wasn't going after any of these goals with love of others as my motivating factor, but I wanted to feel loved and accepted. And the further I walked from the qualities that love possessed, the less I felt love. The facade of perfection was all about me, but it wasn't me at all. I am flawed, and on this earth, that's how I and everyone around me will stay. It was time for me to lay down my expectations and face reality. It was time for me to admit that I couldn't be what I wished I was without God because God was love.

I gave up on the fantasy and got back to reality. I began to lean on God and His ability to change my heart. I concluded that He had a purpose for my life. I can and I will fail at times, but God doesn't stop loving me because of that. I may never become a celebrity here, but I want my life to mean something in eternity. I stopped hustling to gain society's approval and talked again about my struggles and flaws accepting the judgment that others might bestow upon me because of it. I didn't care what others would derive from my social media profile; I was determined to recognize how I made other people feel when they were around me, doing life next to me.

I became aware of my selfishness, but I wasn't out of the weeds just then. I continued to cry out to God in frustration begging Him to help my mental state, but He didn't deliver me in a moment but in many moments. When I felt it was too hard and I was overwhelmed, I cried out again, and again He gave me strength.

God renewed my mind and replaced my cynicism with gratefulness. He reminded me of His love for me and His faithfulness to me. I thanked Him for the prayers He had answered. I thanked Him for an able body to do the laundry and the ability to have children. It was a slow process, but God was faithful.

I can't see the shore, and I don't know what my future looks like, but I am not in the valley anymore. God didn't give me the details of my journey, but He asked me to be faithful along the way. He asked me to keep swimming even when the fog was so thick that I couldn't see how He would accomplish His purposes in me. He asked me to persevere.

Love isn't a game to play; it's a quality we need. It's something our brains and bodies were meant to have. Even though we don't understand love or believe we deserve it, it's still a gift we should accept. Nothing is too much for God to handle; He takes us with whatever baggage we bring. He loves us too much to leave us in that place though.

He will never walk away from you. He has never stopped loving you, and He will always take you back. There was never a time that God didn't want a relationship with you.

No matter what kind of pain you may have had to walk through or are going through now, don't give up. This race can be hard, but don't let it harden your heart. I know you might not be able to see the shore now, but it's right there. This isn't all for nothing. God can use any circumstance for your good and His glory. Will you allow Him to get in the water with you? Do you trust that what He says is truth? I will. I do. And my life is better because of it.

CHAPTER 16

BEFORE, FOR NOW, AND EVER

(Love Never Fails)

David Roever, a purple heart veteran, was a riverboat gunner in the navy during the Vietnam war. An unfortunate event nearly took his life. During a battle, he picked up a phosphorous grenade, but before he could launch it, a sniper shot it out of his hand. David looked down to see the skin from his face lying on his boot and his heart exposed as the phosphorous ate away at every piece of body tissue it touched. David jumped into the water and swam to a helicopter as pieces of his skin and flesh continued to burn off and float alongside him.

When he reached the hospital in Vietnam, they had found that every limb he had was still intact but that sixty pounds of flesh were missing. David was handed a mirror one day so he could look at his face. Horrified, he told himself that no one could ever love someone who looked like him. David unsuccessfully attempted suicide but was committed to trying again.

When he was transferred to the US, the wife of his roommate in the burn unit came to visit him. David said she took one look at her husband, threw her ring on his chest, and told him, "You're embarrassing. I wouldn't walk down the street next to you." David's heart sank. He devised a plan to take his life again but before he could his wife, Brenda, came to visit. She walked in the room ran over to the bed kissed his face and told him she loved him. Brenda's reaction to his state assured David that her love wasn't superficial but unconditional. Her love that day inspired his will to live. David and his wife have been married for over fifty years now.

Metaphorically speaking I've been on both sides of these beds. I've had people look at me and claim I wasn't worthy of their love or attention. I've also experienced undeserved, unconditional love, and sometimes we have to see this sacrificial love to feel it. We have to understand that when our imperfect humanness shows up, we won't be left, and that if it is truly love that's present, they won't; they will want to stand by us through it.

We started with this verse in 1 Corinthians about what love was and explored every area of that definition. Now, we will challenge Jesus on the issue. Did He love despite His circumstances? The cross of calvary would be the ultimate test.

> Humanity was …
> Impatient—Luke 23:35–36 (NKJV): As people stood looking at Jesus on the cross, they mocked Him telling Him to "save Himself" from this terrible death.

Unkind—Luke 22:63–65 (NKJV): They "mocked and beat Him ... struck Him on the face and asked ... 'Who is the one who struck you?'"

Envious—Mark 15:10 (NKJV): "The chief priests had handed Him over because of envy."

Proud—Mark 15:29–32 (NKJV): "Even those who were crucified with Him reviled Him."

Puffed up—Matthew 26:63–66 (NKJV): "He is deserving of death."

Rude—Matthew 27:28–30 (NKJV): "They stripped Him ... twisted a crown of thorns and put it on His head ... they bowed the knee before Him and mocked Him ... they spat on Him took the reed and struck Him on the head ... and lead Him away to be crucified."

Selfish—Matthew 28:15 (NKJV): "Judas, one of Jesus disciples, asked, 'What are you willing to give me if I deliver Him to you?' and they counted out to him thirty pieces of silver."

Provoked—Luke 23:23 (NKJV): "But they were insistent, demanding with loud voices that He be crucified."

Thinking evil—Matthew 26:59–60 (NKJV): "Now the chief priests and elders, and all the council sought false testimony against Jesus to put Him to death, but found none. Even though many false witnesses came forward, they found none."

Rejoicing in iniquity—Luke 23:24 (NKJV): "So Pilate gave sentence that it should be as they requested." Pilate condemned Jesus to death.

Loving lies—Matthew 28:11–15 (NKJV): After Jesus was risen, soldiers were bribed with a large sum of money to say Jesus disciples "came and stole Him away" while the guards slept at the tomb.

Giving up belief—Luke 24:19–20 (NKJV): Jesus's followers began to doubt if He would rise from the dead.

Crushing hope—Luke 24:21 (NKJV): Their hope was being shaken.

Failing to endure—Luke 24:22–24 (NKJV): They had heard, "but Him they did not see."

But God was loving. He never cursed his accusers in the process of His crucifixion. In fact, He cried out, "Father forgive them for they know not what they are doing" (Luke 23:43 NKJV).

Jesus never fought back. He went willingly. He knew what He would have to go through on earth, but He came anyway. He knew what He would have to endure on the cross, but He went anyway.

Isaiah 53:3–7 (NKJV) was written seven hundred years before Jesus's birth, yet it describes what was seen in the verses above. It shows the hate of the human heart but Jesus's love for humanity.

He is despised and rejected by men, a Man of sorrows acquainted with grief. And we hid, as it were, our faces from Him; He was despised, and we did not esteem Him. Surely He has borne our griefs and carried our sorrows; Yet we esteemed Him stricken, Smitten by God, and afflicted. He was wounded for our transgressions, bruised for our iniquities; The chastisement for our peace was upon Him, And by His stripes we are healed. All we like sheep have gone astray; we have turned, everyone, to his own way; And the Lord has laid on Him the iniquity of us all. He was oppressed and He was afflicted, yet He opened not His mouth; He was led as a lamb to the slaughter, and as a sheep before its shearers is silent, So He opened not his mouth.

Jesus was God; He could've stopped the process of His crucifixion and could've declared us unworthy of the sacrifice He was making. But He went through what He went through for us regardless of how it hurt Him. Humans were lost, undone, and without hope, but it was always in God's plan to provide a way out of that through Jesus.

In 1 Corinthians 13:4–8 (NIV), we read,

Love is patient, love is kind. It does not envy, it does not boast, it is not proud. It does not dishonor others, it is not self-seeking, it is not easily angered, it keeps not record of wrongs. Love does not delight in evil but rejoices with the truth. It always protects, it always trusts, always hopes, always perseveres. Love never fails.

Love never fails because it is an act of our will. Jesus Christ is the love of God acted out. He is willing to love you and me, and unlike us, He is able to do it perfectly.

David Roever could have heard his wife's words of love and acceptance and still went along with the decision to end his life.

God offers His love to us in the same way. He says we should believe Jesus was who he said He was,—God—accept and acknowledge that we are who we are— sinners—and receive His love and gift of salvation.

The choice has always been ours; we just don't get to decide what the consequences are. This life wasn't set in motion or designed by us; we don't make the rules, and we don't have to live by them either. That is the beauty and curse of free will.

I truly believe that there is an eternal place of life that humans go after death to be with God and an opposite place without Him of eternal death. If at the end of this life I'm wrong and my body just goes 6ft in the ground, what do I lose? What if I am right though? Eternity is quite literally the biggest gamble in life.

I'll leave you with this conclusion from my own experience.

The God of the bible has changed my life. He's real, I didn't make Him up and I couldn't even if I tried. His story is the most outrageous yet verifiable in existence. The God of the universe sees me, He knows me, He cares about me, and He wants you to have those same assurances. My faith has given me peace during uncertainty, hope during difficulty, and has been my guiding light in the dark. God's love is unlike anything else I've ever experienced. It has defied the weighty displeasures of life and lifted my soul. It's supernatural, out of this world, from another dimension kind of love, and that's why it levitates.

NOTES

Chapter 1: Defining Love

1   "Love," "Definitions from Oxford Languages," google.com.
2   "Love," Merriam-Webster, webster.com.
3   Rachel Simmons, "Why Are Young Adults the Loneliest Generation in America?" *Washington Post*, May 3, 2018, washingtonpost.com.
4   Ecosmith and Jeffery David, "Lonely Generation," Genius, September 26, 2019, genius.com.

Chapter 3: I Mean I'm Kind

1   Cedars-Sinai Staff, "The Science of Kindness." Cedars Sinai, February 13, 2019, cedars-sinai.org.
2   E. P. Sanders and Britannica contributors, "St. Paul the Apostle," April 30, 2020, britannica.com.

Chapter 4: My Heart Bleeds Red, But My Eyes See Green

1   Molly S. Costelloe, "Envy: The Spoiling Emotion," Psychology Today, May 16, 2020, psychologytoday.com.

Chapter 5: Help! I've Fallen and I Can't Get Up

1   David Jeremiah, *David Jeremiah Study Bible*, Worthy Books, November 26, 2013.

Chapter 6: Feeling Bloated? It's Your Salty Self

1   Mayo Clinic Staff, "Narcissistic Personality Disorder," Mayo Foundation for Medical Education and Research, November 18, 2017, mayoclinic.org.
2   History.com, "Adolf Hitler," August 30, 2019, history.com.
3   Lisa Turkest, *Uninvited*, Thomas Nelson, August 9, 2016.
4   David Jeremiah, *David Jeremiah Study Bible*, Worthy Books, November 26, 2013.

Chapter 8: I Fight Like a Girl

1   Ravi Zacharias, Christian Gospel Hype, "Why did God Create the Tree of Good and Evil if He Knew Adam and Eve Would Eat From It?" August 11, 2020, youtube.com.

Chapter 9: Rude Attitude

1   Kendra Adachi, The Lazy Genius Podcast, episode 82: "Loving People You Disagree With," November 2, 2020, applepodcasts.

Chapter 10: The Devil Made Me Do It

1   Independent Imaging, "Use of Contrast Agents in Diagnostic Imaging," independantimaging.com.
2   Maurie Markman, "Stem Cell Transplant for Leukemia." Cancer Treatment Centers of America, IPB, November 5, 2020, cancercenter.com.

Chapter 12: The Truth

1   Kathleen N. Hattrup, "A Doctor on Why 'blood and water' Gushed from Jesus Heart," June 22, 2019, aleteia.org.

2   Matt Perman, "Historical Evidence for the Resurrection," September 12, 2007, desiringgod.org.

Chapter 13: The Whole Truth

1   Elizabeth Howell, "What are the Redshifts and Blueshifts?" space.com.

2   "Causality," *New Scientist*, newscientists.com.

3   "Nothing Existed Before The Big Bang: Stephen Hawking," *Hindustan Times*, March 5, 2018, hindustantimes.com.

4   Stephen Hawking, *The Grand Design*, Bantam, January 1, 2012.

5   Stephen Hawking, *Brief Answers to the Big Questions*, John Murray, January 1, 2018.

6   John Polkinghorne, *One World*, Templeton Press, March 1, 2007.

7   Hugh Ross, "Does a Cosmic Cold Spot Challenge Creation," April 13, 2020, reasons.org.

8   Bart D. Ehrman, *Did Jesus Exist?* HarperOne, March 20, 2021.

9   J. Warner Wallace, "Did Jesus Really Die and Come Back to Life?" September 25, 2020, youtube.com.

Chapter 14: Nothing but the Truth

1   Elizabeth Scott, "What is the Law of Attraction?" November 18, 2020, verywellmind.com.

2   Gordon J. Melton et al., "New Age Movement," April 7, 2016, britannica.com.

3   Steven Bancarz, "The Law Of Attraction Debunked," December 21, 2019, youtube.com.

4   White Chair Films, "I Am Second," iamsecond.com.

5   Nick Vujicic, "Nick Vujicic, Obstacles=Opportunities," 2021, nickvujicic.com.

Chapter 15: So Help Me God

1   Suzanne Raga, "Florence Chadwick, The Woman Who Conquered the English Channel," March 14, 2017, mentalfloss.com.

Chapter 16: Before, for Now, and Ever

1   North Central University, "Dave Roever—Purple Heart Vietnam Veteran Shares His Testimony at North Central University," May 29, 2018, youtube.com.

ABOUT THE AUTHOR

Deanna Block is an author, licensed cosmetologist, artist, wife and mother of three beautiful children. She writes from the small town she grew up in Baudette, MN. Her dynamic personality and artistry make the stories she tells entertaining and tangible. Deanna's desire to connect the mind and the heart appear in her writing by intellectually and spiritually engaging her readers.